SUNNY DANDRIDGE

QUARANTINE
MADE ME DO IT

"AMIDST THE PANDEMIC"

Published by Lee's Press and Publishing Company
www.LeesPress.net

A Premiere Self-Publishing
Services Company

ISBN-13: 978-1-964234-16-8

PAPERBACK

TABLE OF CONTENTS

DEDICATION

To my mother, OC. My backbone, my ride-or-die, my best friend.

Cue and Thai, you mean the world to me.

My sister, who surrounds us as we go about our lives. I have proof she's here with me. She lives forever in our hearts and memories.

My two nieces, the closet things to my sister, are her gifts. Looking at my gorgeous, smart, and independent nieces, I wish I could've seen my worth at their age, and I pray they see theirs.

My Friend Forever Tara, my cheerleader, Class of '91.

Yaw, my realest confidant. Jamaica night school/all-day.

Danielle, we met for a reason. You make me smile, and I love that.

These next two women have inspired me, and they're not even aware. The first encouraged me to finish this book and dream bigger: Reishon "Staxx" Cordero. The second lives her life like it's GOLDEN, and I can taste it: Ayvette Simone Edwards. Both: Class of '91. LAG for LIFE!

I also dedicate this book to al the unarmed Black people who died from police brutality. Please, a moment of silence.

BLACK LIVES MATTER.

1

INTRODUCTION

As this goes to press, a very famous actress is being beaten by her boyfriend. The baby "sleeps" in the other room, and the nanny cam catches everything. Time and time again, we are shocked and startled by the truth.

Just last night, a very handsome and educated man allowed his wife to slap him in the face. Ashamed to tell anyone, yet another victim of domestic violence hides in plain sight.

How do you cover your scars? How do you defend your abuser? How long have you allowed this? Do you allow it? When will it end?

As this goes to press, New York City dedicates November 9th to the Wu-Tang Clan. Celebrating 30 years since their debut album Enter the Wu-Tang (36 Chambers). (1) Let's raise our glasses—Wu-Tang is FOREVER.

Minutes before press time, Bronx native and hip-hop pioneer, KRS-One, sent a very important message via social media, telling anyone interested why he didn't attend this year's Grammy Awards celebrating Hip-Hop's 50 years.

"I carry myself a certain way. I restrict myself in a certain way. I discipline myself in a certain way because I know who I am in this culture. You're in the temple of Hip Hop. This is our home. This place, this institution can never side with, come under, understand the exploitation of our culture. Never will you see me standing in the environment where our culture is being exploited. Or, if you see me there, the next moment this thing's going to fall. I'm there to bring this shit down. If you see me in a situation like that, you should say, 'Yo, watch out! Something's about to happen. Turn your cameras on, something's about to go down. Why's Kris here? Why is he here? Something's about to... he's about to say some shit, right now, that's going to'...you know? Having said that... so when I got the call, I immediately saw—Nah, nah. First of all—it's the Grammys? You get no respect here. None, none, you have no respect here. Now, we respect your existence. We know you exist. And we know that—You're the Grammys. We understand that, and we respect that: your existence. But you ignored hip-hop for forty-nine years. At the 50th year you want to call us? Forty-nine years

2

you ignored us. The 50th year, that's when you call? You couldn't even call on the 47th year and gear it up to at least fifty? Okay? At least get us at forty-seven. No. You wait till the 50th year to want to call Hip-Hop's Authentic Teacher? Nah, you don't get that privilege. I refused to show up. Y'all go ahead and play games with yourselves..."

KRS-One once said, "Rap is something you do, Hip Hop is something you live." It is our culture.

Hip-Hop:

Graffiti. Breakdancing. MC'ing (on the mic), DJing (on the turntables or the 1s and 2s).

Art. Dance. Vocal. Music. Drama. The five components of the Performing Arts.

High School of Music and Art founded by Mayor Fiorella H. LaGuardia in 1936 (school best known for the 1983 classic movie FAME! and subsequently the television show starring Gene Anthony Ray, Debbie Allen, and our Drama teacher, Mr. Moody) became LaGuardia High School of the Performing Arts in the late 1980's. Music and Art was moved from "the Castle on the Hill" to the new, eight-story, air-conditioned, state-of-the-art, LaGuardia HS. Across the street from Martin Luther King Jr. HS, The Juilliard School, and the Arts Library on Amsterdam Avenue.

L.A.G. (not to be confused with the airport, with the same moniker, LGA) #LAGForever!

As this goes to print, there have been more mass shooting in 2023 than days in the year. (3)

Black men comprise 6.1% of the total U.S. population but 25.4% of all the persons killed by law enforcement. (4)

Whether you are pro-second amendment or against it, you must admit America has a problem. And it is that: black and white. Let's talk about it.

3

CHAPTER ONE

Hindsight is 20/20.

HAPPY NEW YEAR!

January 26th, 2020

Kobe and Gianna Bryant lost their lives in a helicopter tragedy along with seven others. (5) The nation mourns The G.O.A.T. (Greatest Of All Time).

February 19th, 2020

Pop Smoke, a 20-year-old New York Rapper, dies at the hands of gun violence. (6)

February 23rd

COVID-19 touches an ill-prepared United States.

February 26th

Katherine Johnson, a 101-year-old Black mathematician who put White men on the moon, will forever be missed. (7) Hidden Figures, starring Taraji P. Henson, brings to light the struggles of being an intelligent Black woman in the 1950s.

March 13th

Right before dawn Friday morning, Breonna Taylor was startled out of her sleep thinking her home was being ambushed. At the same time multiple police officers with no body cameras rammed her door in with a "No Knock" raid. Not knowing who burst through the door, she looked to her legally armed boyfriend to protect her. He shot once. They "shot blindly" and killed Breonna. (8)

March 15th

Self-quarantine imposed on Westfield, New Jersey. Residents are given an 8pm curfew.

Sitting in bed, I journal:

April Fucking-Fool's Day 20-20!

2 weeks under quarantine, and another estimated 4 weeks to go, and I'm not even kidding—the coronavirus has shut down the world! New York and New Jersey have been hit the hardest. Travel bans, schools closed, malls, movie theaters, bars, and restaurants are only for take-out or delivery. Crazy people are hoarding toilet paper and paper towels. STAY INDOORS! We're under national lockdown. We are being asked to self-quarantine amidst the pandemic. Curfew has been set to 8pm as millions are out of work.

April 9th

The Ring Doorbell app alerted my phone of a shooting investigation nearby. The alert read: The WPD is investigating a shooting near the intersection of State St. & Ayers Court at approximately 3am on April 9th, 2020. We are requesting any videos from the area, which may show the suspect's vehicle. Please forward any information to DTony@ the Westfield Police Department.

April 10th

A text I received linked me to a newspaper article:

HEADLINE: Woman, 25, Charged with Attempted Murder in Westfield

Authorities charged a 25-year-old woman with attempted murder in two separate shootings that they said occurred hours apart in Westfield. Tabitha Dunkin, of Westfield, first fired at the intended victim, also 25, and missed in the area of Tryon Avenue and Washington Place shortly after 11pm Wednesday, authorities said.

She fled in a silver-colored Mercedes-Benz. Around 3am Thursday, Dunkin again in Westfield shot at the victim, who was in a vehicle heading west on East Dean Street. She missed her target again and instead wounded the driver in the shoulder. He was taken to Parkside Hospital, where he was treated before being released. Lieutenant Martin Green of WPD released a statement, "An Englewood sergeant arrested Dunkin with a loaded 9mm handgun."

Westfield police have charged Dunkin with two counts of attempted murder, as well as making terroristic threats, criminal intent, and weapons offenses. She remains held in the Bourdon County Jail pending court action.

Additional charges are pending in the case, which remains under investigation.

(All names have been changed to protect the innocent or daresay innocent.)

Karim

10:30pm

Were you the intended target?

I think you know the answer to that but its okay for her to hide that my brother tryna fuck her but not okay for me to dump her & not wanna talk

Crazy to hear this.
Is the driver ok?

She admitted to being down to fuck my brother but he can tell me to leave her and not tell me that. best ever reason to leave. He took that bullet and as far as I'm concerned he deserved it. My brother was the driver. Only reason he's not dead was he leaned over to open the passenger door cuz the bullet went thru the headrest. But he coulda not tried to fuck my bitch and be part of why I didn't trust her lol. Lik should I feel bad? He did me dirty and so did she. I was lucky to be missed but he got hit lol thats karma lik a mf

Karim

Wow
Benjamin & I said your
relationship would have
made a great reality TV
show.
Too soon?
Sorry

2:59am

Benjamin would rather have her
and the kids there and pay me
for baking soda. Sorry I was on
the phone I never cared ...lol
she was a means to an end. She
can tell y'all that she got a
second boyfriend but not me
and it's not lik yall cared. Why
tell Karim he is a fool...this
drama is great tv, right?

"Pay me for baking
soda"?
Yoooo! LOL! What?

Yea, cuz he thinks powder is
stronger cuz it hurt when the
real shit is smooth lol. I've been
giving him full grams of arm and
hammer and he said he felt a
drip lol

7

I knew that shit burnt too much!

I hate him that's why I just take his money. Cuz his problem makes me more but idk how u addicted to bakin soda

He said the rock which is real coke feels weaker lol
His dumb ass convinced himself so I didn't argue
I'm glad u got away from him before he ruined u

I think he's in love with her

Cuz he told me Tabitha was gonna call me from his phone so don't answer and I'm lik why is she there...
Why would u let her even do that
He is
He can have her in 8 to 10 lmao

Oh shit!

Karim

I'ma do this line and take a shot
for Tab's crazy ass
And also a line for fuckin my
brother
So 2 lines
But she try to kill me lol And hit
my bro by accident
who added to the issue in the
first place lol...I love it
God is good

> She said you beat her

She also said she didn't cheat on
me while I scroll thru her phone
showing her pussy and getting
dick pics

> She said you dragged
> her out her house

How. Her pop and nana
would've heard that

> Crazy it's just crazy

Cuz u told Ben you
needed some "white girl"
to stay up for homework
but failed all classes
No1 can be trusted

Karim

Never liked her

But why should I have to lose
my life cuz she lied
Lol
How does that even out

You need therapy
sweetie. Maybe not
this week but soon

I just used her to be
around Ben to make
money and smoke his
weed...she would buy
bottles and leave them in
my car to drink yall shit
I don't need therapy
U think this is the first
time I got shot at?

To find peace

Niggas don't lik it wen u
steal they drugs so I'd
shoot me too

lol

How do I need therapy
for knowing better
and never trusting her

Karim

I found peace seeing her
mugshot bcuz she coulda killed
me and then got arrested but
she didn't get her wish and
gotta face the music and u can't
confuse shooting at me as love
So I dnt feel bad for the kids no
one

                    Must got that good D

Same way Ben would ask
me for advice... bring u in
his house with a room
full of gifts & shit for
another girl lik a fuckin
dumass I know better
I used to advise him on
you too
And still too dum to
know when coke burns
it's not coke or not pure

                    He tries to look happy
                    but he's miserable

My dick makes bitches
shoot when I leave
lol so yes it is good
It's so good she can cheat
on me and still be mad

Karim

I'm leavin lik she innocent

> Oh that night was memorable. His room looked like a Valentine's gift shop

But couldn't respect you enough to move it. U was there not the girl they was for lol he so dum

> Yes. Learned a lot that night. Never look back

He never is happy... he will cop and tell us to come and share everything for company.
Lol
Tabitha spent the day at his house after I got off work Tuesday when we had plans By this time Wednesday I was being shot at 6xs
Lol

> Do you have a gun?

12

Cuz she made sure I heard her tell Ben they meant to be and she should be with him lol while I'm standing here right. He just let her talk lookin at me lik a pussy lol

But since u up and I'm grateful I'm alive. Can't sleep... u wanna smoke?

He's an ass cuz I told him don't get in the middle Hmmmmm

Yea why not

I have no guns

I can't smoke in my apartment

1290 west boulder

Ok gimme 15 mins

Blunt or joint?

Blunt

13

Karim

And pull up in the driveway next to my car I'll start rolling but can we smoke in your car cuz my seat full of glass lol

> Ok

Bet see u soon. It's a beige house. And I dnt have corona lol I had to be tested to keep working

> Lol
> OMW

I'm serious, lol this shit is real booboo

3:15am

Wya

> Sorry I'm in my car now

Okay I thought u was setting me up to kill me next
Lol

Karim

Not funny!

Are you really in the car lol

3:24am

I'm here

CHAPTER TWO

I met Karim and Tabitha in Benjamin's backyard late summer of 2019. I've known Benjamin for ten-plus years. He was in his late 20s and I was in my mid-30s. In 2008, we met on a site called NoStrings.com.

It was lust at first sight. Cinnamon brown, tall with a handsome boy face and perfect teeth. He smiled constantly. I loved that about him...along with him being a perfect gentleman and a book enthusiast (he droned on about science fiction the most), he had an elephant-sized penis. The only bad thing was there was no way I could see him on a regular basis. Just the thought of my skin expanding to endure his slow methodical strokes. Broke my heart when I envisioned myself explaining to my future husband, years from now, that I didn't have any more muscle memory.

After about six months, I found out he wanted four children, names all starting with the letter "B." Having two teenage sons, I knew I was done having babies. I broke up with him. I let him go find his future wife and have their future family. Benjamin Jr., Brooklyn, and the twins, Beatrice, and Bert. I liked him too much to stand in his way of happiness. Little did I know, he would continue living in his mother's basement apartment, childless, and content with her cooking and providing for him. (Carl Jung explains this as the "man-child.")

Early 2019, Benjamin posted something on Instagram about "wake n bake," and I was intrigued (Wake n bake: when one smokes marijuana upon waking up). We spoke through DM for a few weeks, and then I saw him. After all these years, I still haven't found a man with as much girth as him. Instead of just fuckbuddies, we wanted to try something different. So, he suggested we explore a real relationship and do more things actual couples do. We made a list:

1) Meet friends and family

2) Have dinners out

3) Movies three times a month or, at least, commit to watching the last three seasons of The Big Bang Theory together.

Since meeting friends was the first on the list, he arranged a get together.

Initially, I didn't think anything about Karim. He was arrogant. An alpha, opposite of Benjamin, a bully of a drug dealer. He sniffed as much as he sold and always carried an open bottle of Tanqueray. At five foot seven, Karim stood inches underneath Benjamin's six foot two. He had a honey caramel complexion, sharp features, and a wild afro. Attractive enough except he reeked of all-day and last night.

Karim and Tabitha were already there when I arrived. They were sitting to the left of Benjamin, so, naturally, I sat to the right. That became "my seat" all summer, which was cool with me because it gave me the vantage point of who walked in.

Tabitha was between the guys, so we met face-to-face. She looked sleepy. She would flash her teeth in response to laughter, the only way I knew she was listening. I didn't know if she was genuinely engrossed in her phone or if she was just using it as a distraction. When she did look up, I could see she was pretty: hair in curls, thick bone structure with beautiful cocoa brown skin.

Karim was funny. We laughed with him, and we laughed at him as we drank and smoked weed, which felt like all night. After my second glass of E&J and Pepsi and I'm sure his twelfth swig from the bottle, he flirted with me. I remember noticing Tabitha continued to divert her attention from my direction.

Keith, Karim's brother, and this other guy, Daysun, came later. Keith, milk chocolate, short afro, wore glasses was obviously Karim's wingman. Whenever Karim talked, Keith agreed and nodded with excitement. Daysun's thin frame was darkened by his hoodie. He clapped his hands often in conversation and ended every other sentence with, "Word as Bond!" (Hip Hip lingo meaning he always speaks the truth.)

If I had to guess he was no older than twenty-six. Not one of them looked over thirty, but Daysun stood out as being the educated one on world events. He was an activist and outspoken about Black issues, history, with a major in political street science. I recall laughing when we first were introduced *because when he pronounced his name, I associated it with Dijon mustard. When I repeated it back to him in sheer confusion, "Dayjon?", he smiled and said, "I like that! I like that! Makes me sound French and shit." We all laughed.*

In a comedy with a soundtrack Karim was the main character; he took the spotlight. Must admit, I like a dominant male who's funny and supplies drugs. I'm simple and easy like that. Once the alcohol took over the tongue; we started in on the Yo Mama jokes. But before too long, I sliced him down with a quirky-worded insult. The guys groaned and laughed. Tabitha showed her teeth a few times as I clapped my hands twice. I love a good slice. He became argumentative with a smile and wanted to make the guys groan again but for him this time. I sat back and let the smile die down before coming back with another quick-witted insult. He and I got into a debate, and the others chimed in. Benjamin would yell, "Baby?!" when my not-so-nice observations were literally the truth. It was also funny to watch someone think of a comeback.

Whatever we were talking about gave way to a whole new nighttime ritual. Karim and I dominated the conversation. Tabitha looked on quietly while Benjamin became my "wingman." It was a good night. After everyone left, I slept over and we "watched a movie," or so we said...

The next time all his friends and I sat around in the backyard forum, Karim wasn't there. Tabitha was able to take the stage. She apologized I had to meet her "all fucked up like that." She was different. Not just because she wasn't wearing her wig. It was as if she wanted to say, "Now that he's not here..."

She spoke confidently and stood strong in her conviction to make anyone listen. She had a rough childhood, and her word was her bond. If you believed everything that she said, she would have you believe she was a hard-working, independent mother of three.

The first time I got to talk to her without a stiff buzz. She bragged out of loving care for her babies. "My boys," She shook her head, "I would die for my children; each boy has a piece of my heart." She didn't care how many neighbors called the Division of Youth and Family Services on her. She was proud; she fought and won all six cases.

Tabitha intrigued me at first because her brand of humor was different, and I didn't know whether to entertain her stories as factual or delusional. They sounded like a little bit of both. I remember thinking, "This girl is crazy!" several times. She would tell stories of traveling from state to state and even selling drugs internationally. A small fragment of her reminded me of me at twenty-something years old, if I'd had my three boys at 25, talked incessantly, and never learned early on that your kids need you at night, too. We could have been sisters, well, more like auntie and niece.

I would try to get a word in edgewise, but Tabitha's flow of verbal diarrhea didn't stop often enough. I learned early, when she was by herself, you had to jump in to speak - the opposite of when Karim was around.

Benjamin despised Karim and only stomached him for his relationship with Tabitha. Ben swore up and down that he and Tab only slept together a few times years ago and that it was nothing to worry about. I knew Ben wasn't a big fan of Karim and would gossip about him and Tabitha being the next VH1 reality show: Sex Drugs and Hip Hop/ The Jersey Edition. He told me about a night a few weeks before; they were having an argument and not speaking. The entire time, they sat right next to each other and texted each other under the table.

Ben would sound protective of her and defend her when she would leave with Keith. He was sure they were good friends and lived a few blocks down in the same direction, so they would "just walk home together." I didn't think anything of their kinship until the night she told him, "Slow up, I'm coming." I especially became aware of her fondness for him when Karim wasn't around. At first, she just appeared intoxicated and in need of assistance walking home. After a few weeks, it appeared she was desperate for nighttime company. Then again, so did Karim.

I wore dresses in the summer and to our backyard gatherings. Karim frequently made me feel as if I had just bent over and my hem was too high. His eyes spoke lust. I could feel his intensity and wondered how Benjamin felt with a man outwardly ogling his woman. Karim was a fast talker and very attractive. I couldn't decipher if I was taking him seriously or just enjoying the attention. He held my eye contact, and I remember laughing and feeling pretty in front of his girlfriend.

19

One Friday afternoon, we all got there early, and I was standing next to him. Innocently, his arm brushed against me, and he yelled, "Oh, I'm so sorry. I touched your breast! I didn't mean to. Excuse me? Benjamin, please excuse me. I didn't mean to touch your girlfriend's breast with my hand..." He made us all laugh, especially me. I was giggling like an eighth-grade schoolgirl. After the third time he caught my eye and smiled, I shot him a look as if to say, stop it, which only intrigued him more. He was witty; he had a dry and mean sense of humor. He didn't care who he offended while he flaunted his pocket full of twenties.

It was difficult picturing him and Tabitha as a couple. She was shy around him, just stared at her phone the whole time, acting as if not to notice. That night, for some reason, she left without him. I knew I wasn't the only one who noticed Karim's unspoken lust and that night I played with it. I stood up to give him a hug when he and Keith went to leave and I said, "I want a full-frontal hug." Only because Tabitha wasn't there, he tried to kiss me, and I slapped him. Twice. I heard a gasp from the crowd, and I remember laughing out loud. After sitting down, I mumbled, "As if!" for Benjamin's sake since he was sitting right there.

Karim acted stunned and walked away slowly, holding his face with his open bottle of liquor. He said something like, "Git your girl!" He stared and smiled in my direction as I mocked his defeat with my facial expressions.

I knew after that...I wanted him to kiss me.

He apologized the next time we were all together, and I remember looking directly at Tabitha when he said he tried to kiss me. He blamed it on the alcohol. Karim laughed and spoke in a southern ragtime voice, "Cuz sometimes I be outta pocket, see? I be ova here, and the pocket be ova there. See? I'm ova here and the pocket be way ova there... Pocket there, and I'm here." This was a routine he would do quite often to explain his weird and sometimes careless behavior. Keith and Benjamin laughed along with him. I waited for Tabitha's reaction. It was cold and aloof. I couldn't help laughing; it was funny. He kept saying it. "I'ma ova here-pockets ova there..." sounding like Sammy Davis, Jr. or Chubby Checker. You couldn't help but laugh.

We would get together at least three times a week. I spent most of the late summer of 2019 with them. I wasn't working, lived with my mother, drove the car I already paid off, and spent my child support money on food, clothes, and drugs. My mother didn't make me pay rent, so I was "living the life" as "they" would say.

I would ask Benjamin if he needed anything from the store. Anything from cigarettes to cigarillos to liquor, I would pick it up. I felt as if my manners wouldn't be up-to-par if I didn't. It was obvious these people weren't bringing anything to the table, except for Karim, who would always have his open bottle. They would sometimes "match" with Ben on the weed. But most of the time Keith, Tabitha, Daysun, and this new girl, Daisy, who would pop up randomly, would show up empty-handed.

He was just pleased everyone came and had a good time, always smiling. He didn't pay his mother rent either, and, little did she know, she was hosting the parties. Red cups, sodas, bottled water, and ice every night. He thanked me for inspiring him to get another job at Stop N' Shop. He worked there every other evening, and at Family Dollar most mornings and weekends to close. His license was suspended, and for three thousand dollars, he could get it back. But his paychecks went to drugs and alcohol instead.

I looked for the logic but couldn't find any, anywhere. He was allowing his friends to use him, and he wasn't concerned about paying down his fine. He was fully aware, and it didn't bother him, but it disturbed me.

August 2019

Tabitha and I bonded one night when it was just the three of us. She told Ben and I a story involving intense love and drug travel. Her details included passionate lovemaking and the true depth of betrayal as their romance ended in money laundering, a mixture of threesomes, and the man she thought she loved showing his true colors. I listened with excitement and wondered how this girl so young had lived a life so much older than her years. I was reminded of a recent breakup I had endured worth recalling for midnight story time.

"It's crazy because I feel as if I lived through a similar situation a few months ago when I met this guy online, and we started dating..." I turned

21

to Ben and asked, "Is it ok if I share this story with her?" I mean, it had just happened, and he was there for me as a shoulder.

He nodded and answered, "Yea."

February 2019

King Shaburger. I should've been alerted by his affiliation with a group known for lifting Black men from prison to self-awareness. It was more of a cult than a religious or African study group. The "father" of the tribe prided himself on picking Black men up from prison, drug addiction, gang violence, and slavery to a knowledge of self. The Black man is seen as Supreme, no one higher. You were encouraged to change your name and embrace a name fit for a King or a God. Shaburger taught me about the number system, each having a meaning and each day having a new inscription known as Mathematics. In turn, the alphabet also had its own meaning. Knowledge meant a better sense of consciousness for the few five percent of the population that understood the truth. But how do you tell someone they're in a cult? You can't.

He was recently released from prison, with multiple charges. He told me to "guess" when I asked which ones.

"Guns?"

"Yea—"

"Drugs?"

"Yea—"

"Trespassing?"

"Yea—"

"Robbery?"

"Yea—"

"Aggravated assault? Drug trafficking?"

"Yea! Why? You the police?"

"No, just curious..." What could imprison someone for 27 consecutive *years? My mind only wandered; my next two guesses were probably better left unanswered.*

August 2019

"We dated hard and fast. He wanted to spend all of our free time together. He didn't drive but would travel back and forth from Brooklyn on the train and bus to see me. I loved that. I knew full well about his years in prison, but I took his word of self-knowledge as rehabilitation. He met my sons, we took a trip to Vegas, and even spoke of marriage."

"What happened to him?" As Tabitha anxiously awaited the twist and said corruption.

"So, one night, I drove to Brooklyn to spend the night. We got drunk, and he accused me of cheating because my pH levels were off. It was right after my period. I had a stronger odor than usual. He's back and forth with 'Who is it?', 'What's his name?', and 'How long has this been going on?' And then finally, I'm like, 'Fine! I'm cheating!' He's instantly enraged and yells, 'So, why are you here?' I look around and answer, 'Good question!' So, I get up to leave and he grabs me back. Straight off, he's sorry, didn't mean to scare me because at that point, I'm crying and telling him to get off of me. He begs me not to leave, and I love a man that begs, so I stay until the morning. But I planned to leave and not come back. He was way too aggressive and belligerent for me. In the morning, when I gather my things to leave, he decides he wants a ride to Jersey, so I have to wait. Anyway, long story short, I broke up with him. He starts calling, begging, leaving messages, and once he realizes I blocked his number, he starts calling from other people's phones and using other people's numbers."

Tabitha looked stunned, shaking her head in disbelief.

"Yea!" I continued, "One message came in from an unknown number, and it was so evil, ugly, and threatening—the person whose phone it was texted me back a few minutes later, apologizing. Saying they didn't know the guy, but somebody just asked to borrow their phone and they felt bad that someone would use their phone to talk to me like that."

"Whoa-?"

"I knew that I would need to speak to him for him to move on, but he insisted we talk in person. We had broken up before, and he'd used this tactic to get me back the last time. I was fed up and knew I deserved a man who wasn't bipolar. I kept firm. A week had gone by, and I thought he moved on. Until one night, he comes to my house unannounced..."

"How did he have your address?"

"He wanted to send me flowers for Valentine's Day—"

"Ah, man!" Tabitha and I had broken off from Benjamin, who heard the story before and had become enthralled in his tablet.

"Yea...so he's begging me to come out for just a minute. He loves me and just wants to talk. 'Please, baby, don't leave it like this. I just need to see you. I miss you and I love you. I promise I will never hurt you again. I took an Uber all this way...baby, please.' But the reason I blocked him in the first place was because he showed me crazy—"

"What do you mean?" She said squinting.

"He would text me pictures of the toilet and say he just threw up, saying he's been crying all night. He can't sleep, eat, or work because he's so devastated. The pictures of the toilet were over the top for me. I couldn't have him disturb my day like that."

I recalled the night he came to my house and lured me outside. When I didn't want to kiss or hug him, he became combative and tried grabbing my phone when I glanced down at it to locate the emergency call button. He pushed me against the hood of my car and proceeded to beat me over the head and face with his wrist.

"His wrist?"

"Yea, not your fist—you can hurt yourself like that. His wrist." I showed her the inner part of my arm. "The base of the hand—it's harder and has fewer moving parts, so you avoid breaking bones or swollen knuckles."

Tabitha shook her head as I realized for the first time, she was intently listening to me.

"He beat me in front of my house. I was screaming for help, but no one heard. Finally, I just threw my phone down." I made a wide, over-the-head movement. "Because he kept saying, 'Gimme your phone, bitch!' So, he let me go and when he reached down, I ran to the house. I was screaming for someone to call 9-1-1. My sons were there, but one had headphones on, playing 2K and the other one had just stepped out of the shower. All they wanted to do was go outside and hurt this nigga. I couldn't blame them, but I couldn't let them go either. Fucking crazy-ass man. Who the fuck knows what the fuck this nigga might do? I called the cops. They came quickly. They couldn't find him—they looked at bus stops, thinking he was walking around the neighborhood. I knew they weren't going to find him. He probably dipped into someone's backyard. But now they want to take me to the hospital cuz I'm bleeding. I go. I have a mild concussion and he fractured my nose. While I'm sitting in the hospital being questioned by police, one of them gets a call over the radio that the 'perp' is back at the house, attempting to get in. I scream, 'WHAT THE FUCK!?' The officers try to calm me down and let me know they're handling the situation. Thank God my family stayed home instead of coming with me. That nigga tried to throw a brick and a garbage can through my window. They had to call the cops again."

"I can't believe this—this is a crazy-ass story. Are you alright? What happened?" Tabitha was delighted by the story, she grinned without teeth this time. A smirk followed by an extended eyebrow raise.

"They called the K-9 unit this time and found this nigga around the corner slumped in a bush. He didn't break anything because my mother just installed triple pane windows that can't be broken. Thank God! We found out the next morning that he went around back, found a spray can, and tried to set my basement door on fire! He probably burned himself, that stupid motherfucker!

"Last summer, mom installed a flame-retardant door at the same time she updated the windows." I let out a "Pssst..." and a loud, "HA! They arrested him, he got three months in county, and I got a permanent restraining order—and I applied for my gun license. They told me this wasn't his first domestic violence case. The only difference was I was the only one who went through with pressing charges. He'll get out at the beginning of 2020..."

"I got my glock last week. Did you get a gun yet?"

"No, not yet. I'm still waiting for the paperwork to go through. That motherfucker called me collect from jail already..." She shook her head in disbelief and came in closer to the table; she lowered her voice to a whisper as her advice was coveted.

"Be careful. He might get out early...and if he's stupid enough to come back, call me."

We were fully engaged and totally forgot we were sitting next to Benjamin and in that split second, I felt her gaze. There was a moment of silence in which I nodded and felt her sentiment.

April 10th, 2020, 3:15AM

"So, what the fuck happened?" I asked after he showed me the bullet hole in his passenger door. I couldn't help but see the one in the windshield. When I got into his driver's seat, I noticed the angle of the shot. A couple of millimeters to the right and the bullet would've easily ended his life.

We sat in my Wrangler to smoke. I learned he didn't just send the article to me but to everyone in his contacts. He said I was the only one who responded. "It must've been the D." I knew my comment was original and would get me where I am now.

I laughed and said, "No doubt, but what the fuck happened?"

"She crazy. That's all." Karim responded.

"So that night..." I continued to press him.

"Yeah, I was supposed to just meet her and talk."

"Who said 'talk?' Did she say talk, or did you say talk?"

"She said she wanted to talk because I was breaking up with her. She finally admitted to me, my brother and her were hooking up for sex for weeks, maybe even a few months. I told her we were over, and she wanted to talk, and when she got out of the car, I saw the gun in her hand and I was like, 'How you come to talk to me wit a gun?'"

"What did she say?" His cool demeanor intrigued me.

He pulled on the blunt, mouth full of smoke. "She ramblin' on 'bout how I always play the victim when it's been her cheating this whole time."

"Oh, yeah! I heard about your ex—"

"That was common knowledge. She knew about that too—that wasn't nothing new. She was upset because my brother and her got busted."

"You caught them having sex?"

"No, but she finally admitted all the text messages with Keith were to set up a fuckin' place. I broke up with her, told her I didn't want anything to do with her, and she come to my house with a gun. The same gun I took her to get a couple of weeks ago in Paterson. The same one she tried to kill me with." He lit a cigarette and handed me the blunt. "I got out the car to talk to her."

"Wait! You got out knowing she had a gun?"

"Yeah, I said, 'Fuck it!' Either I'm taking a bullet, and this bitch goes to jail, or she misses and goes to jail. Either way, she's going to jail."

I smiled and gazed deeply into his eyes and tried to see how this man was so calm after he went through all of that. And for the first time since I met him, he smiled longer than two seconds. He seemed genuinely at peace, and I found a friend in his eyes. I already knew I wanted to fuck him, but right then I knew it was going to be good. He talked as I imagined him on top of me. He made the story funny, and he continued to make fun of Ben. I laughed because it was true, and since Ben and I broke up two months ago, I wanted to let Karim know the cookies were in the bag.

It worked. Right then, he reached for my face. He shocked me when he leaned over the center console. Once close enough, I could smell his essence. He was freshly showered. He paused and said, "You want me to kiss you, don't you?" I remember blushing, giggling gleefully, and willingly agreeing. His closeness made me tickle. Like a nine-year-old girl in the backroom with a seven-year-old boy and everybody else in the front. I wanted to grab him and suck his face, but I didn't. I understood he was showing restraint—a sign of a true gentleman. I cautioned myself not to fall in love with him, even though I knew my track record with bad boys and dangerous situations. I could not, under any circumstances, fall in love. Tabitha would get out of jail and kill me. I smiled to myself and leaned further into the kiss.

Summer of '19

Benjamin escorted me to my car every night. I parked in front of his house, so he walked me to the street, and we kissed. Benjamin liked several little kisses with a noise of kisses in between. Karim walked by and came close enough for inspection. I think I remember hearing a soft moan and he said, "See? That's what I need. You got a sister? Or a friend, like you?"

"No. No one's like me."

"I know, but not even a cousin or...a mentor..."

I laughed out loud. I couldn't help myself. I liked him. With a smile on my face, I kissed Benjamin a few more times and said, "See you Tuesday?"

"K."

Karim continued, "Com' on, I need somebody like you, like older. Help me out."

As I pulled my door open and looked over my shoulder, my eyes locked with Tabitha's in the car across the street, a few feet back. Damn! I wondered, were her windows open?

April 10th, 2020, 4:44AM

Karim asked, "Did you come over to see?"

"See whaa?" I looked around.

"See what drove that bitch crazy?"

"Well, I already know you were taking care of her and driving her and her kids around. She loved y—"

"Shhhhh..." He held his fingers to my face, "Did you come to see or nah?"

I was smiling too hard to speak, so I nodded. He was close enough to *kiss me, and I wanted him to, so I inched in closer to touch his nose with mine. I shook my face to rub our nose tips together and laughed. He thinks I'm cute. I can see it in his eyes. Then, finally, he did. It was more of a bottom-lip suck, so I repositioned my top lip to suck his. I took control and bit his bottom lip a little. His demand for control dominated my desire to feel soft and relaxed in his grasp. He had my face and full attention. I closed my eyes and breathed in his scent of soap and—what's that? A light hint of cigarette/socks? That's when I realized I was hooked.*

After about 27 seconds of passionate tongue kissing with eyes closed and light moans he pushed me back in my seat with his full palm right against my throat. My shift in weight revealed to me I was wet, and I wanted him to know. The moan was unintentional, except when he clamped down on my windpipe, I gasped for more air. I grabbed his hand to release his pressure momentarily, as I wanted that hand to feel the rest of my body. I had jonesed for him for a long time now, and the fact it took Tabitha going to jail to allow this to happen excited me. A great number of things excited me at that moment. Our age difference, his bravado, the weed, and my moisture put it over the edge. Right then, I wanted him to know I wasn't wearing any panties.

April 8th, 10:45PM

He dipped behind the Preschool on Tryon Avenue, he swerved in front of the 7-Eleven, he reversed and then accelerated past her on Dean Street— she shot twice. The first bullet went through the windshield hitting the rearview mirror. The second put a hole in the passenger door. The explosion of glass made him swerve again and almost hit a parked car. When he lost control, he slammed the brakes down hard. The rudder burned marks in the road. The Hyundai Sonata sat at the green light as he looked around expecting the worst. The burnt tires created a fog around him, and headlights cast an eerie shadow overhead.

The street was empty as far as he could see. The intense ringing in his ears blurred his vision and made him shake his head for relief. Seconds later, he saw her U-turn on State Street without brakes and heard the wheels screech loudly. Now headed towards him, she took aim out the open window.

The block was quiet as he hunched down in the front seat. The adrenaline made him accelerate in the pedestrian walkway. She shot and missed, hitting the blue mailboxes on the corner. He suddenly stopped short to maneuver the turn onto West Boulder. He drove erratically through stop signs without much thought. After driving three blocks, he dimmed his lights to parking and slowed to just below the speed limit. He threw the car in park, looked over his shoulder as he walked up the stairs to his house.

Tabitha came down the street the wrong way with no lights and quickly sped past him. He turned, looked at her and motioned, what. He saw her brake lights at the intersection and knew she was coming back.

Once inside, Karim got Keith on FaceTime, "Yo, Eif! THIS BIG DUMB BITCH JUST TRIED TO FUCKIN KILL ME. Can you believe this bitch?!"

"What the FUCK?!"

"She shot three times! DOWN THE FUCKING BLOCK WITH THE GLOCK I GOT HER!"

"You home?!?'

"Yea!" Karim breathing deeply.

"Yo, bro! FUCK THAT BITCH! I'm on my way."

"Bringdafuckinheat."

"Wit-out question."

11:45PM

Through tears and clamped teeth Tabitha yelled, "I SHOT THA MuddaFUCKIN' BAST-ARD!"

Benjamin held quiet, lit a cigarette, and wanted less to do with her right now. He watched her as she paced outside in his mother's alleyway. He knew he could be an accessory to murder if she killed him. So, he asked, "Did you get him?" He scratched his head, nervously awaiting her answer.

She shook her head with tears running down her face. "What should I do now? Can I stay here?"

"Ummm--my mom's home right now...maybe you should go home, try to chill..."

She didn't let him finish, "I gotta go get him!"

"You should go home!"

"No! I'll be back! I love you!" Tabitha said as ran back to her grandmother's Mercedes-Benz GLC 300.

"Love you too!" Not knowing this would be the last time he saw her.

January 22nd, 2020

I broke it off. We talked on the ride home from Applebee's (#2 on the dating list) after my birthday dinner. I merely stated we were headed on opposing courses in our lives— something I should've realized going into our non-purposeful union. He said I broke his heart. I said, if we kept going, we would've been going nowhere because he's content where he is. I started working a different schedule, went back to school online. I'd just moved into my place and wanted him to grow with me. I used his words against him. He told me he wanted to retire from Family Dollar and live with his mother until she dies, so she'd leave him and his siblings the house. House divided by three equals him being able to afford a condo in Port Jefferson overlooking New York. His financial obligations didn't rush him because, as he said, "I would just be getting my license back, and there's no real rush to drive."

"You want to stay there?" I asked him on my birthday. "Please do. But I gotta go." It was kinda harsh at the moment and I regretted saying it as soon as I drove away. But in hindsight, I wanted him for the yeti penis and nothing more. (Yeti Penis: hard to find and elusive. An attractive and committed man with a somewhat deformed and enlarged penis.)

Valentine's Day

On IG I posted:

Happy _alentine's _ay

For those of you not getting any V or D tonight.

Moments later Benjamin liked it. Not being sexually active since we broke up, I was intrigued he gravitated toward my innuendo. I needed further clarification. I texted first.

Benjamin

11:38pm

You home alone?

Yes

Me too

Did you want to come over & smoke

Cool be there shortly

When I arrived, we smoked in my Jeep. It wasn't raining, but it was cold, and his mother had just installed the Ring DoorCam on her front and side doors. He didn't want to alert her phone to watch him smoke. He said he had some things for me, so we walked toward the house. It was awkward walking in; I almost wanted to cover my face. When I reached the bottom of the all-too-familiar basement staircase, I was hit with a—Valentine Love Shop. He had heart balloons, a huge teddy bear with "I Love You" etched in the heart it was holding, and an oversized shiny red bag. I shook my head in disbelief because if they were for me, he would've yelled surprise or something like that.

He was mumbling, and I said, "Wow! Someone must love you," thinking the gifts were from somebody else.

"My mom and my sister love me very much…"

I thought for a moment. His mom and sis wouldn't show love like this. I looked in the bag and saw there was nail polish, no-show socks, candy, and other little things girls love from the dollar store.

Both of his futon beds were full. The one we would primarily sit and sleep on had books and papers dumped on it, making it difficult to sit there. So, I was forced to sit next to the stuffed animal. He was cute and extra soft. I got close, and then before I noticed, I was snuggling with it. I didn't want to let go until I thought, he never did this for me. I said it, too.

"You never did this for me!"

He lied, "You never gave me a chance."

"What do you mean…My housewarming, Christmas, my birthday? I got a Dove soap set and a bottle."

"I'm sorry. I didn't mean to hurt you with this, but I didn't want to hide anything either."

I said nothing and focused on the television. I became really invested in Family Guy, and since I love Stewie, I stayed. Once the episode ended, I jumped up and yelled, "Okay, gotta go!"

I was insulted by the invitation especially since it was all intended for another girl. He said she couldn't come tonight but would see her tomorrow. Tiffany's her name. He had all of those gifts for her—and what did he have for me? A few things I left at his house along with my panties he would tuck away each time I spent the night. Was this slight in virtue revenge for the "heartbreak"? I walked away in single dumbfuckness (when you feel at one with your newfound fucked-up situation). I haven't seen him in person since then. I unfollowed him when he wanted to be seen at the beach with Tiffany.

"Hello"

"Hey what's up with your girl?"

"She just got fed up, I guess."

"And she was at your house, and you saw the gun?"

"I mean, I saw the gun, but I didn't know she was going to use it."

"Did you try to talk her down?"

"She's a grown woman and—he got what he deserved."

"And what was that?"

"A busted-out windshield and a fucked-up night."

"Oh. Okay. I see. You didn't help your friend see the flaw in her plan? That she would get locked up and taken away from her children and destroy her and her grandparents' life?" He stuttered and slurred his words like he was talking to himself out loud. I couldn't believe this spineless man used to stand before me.

"Thank God she didn't kill anyone!"

"Yea—" he said quietly.

"Especially you—because you could've been an accessory to murder..." I said.

"...Yea."

"So, why do you sound like you were rooting for her? You don't care much about him, huh?"

"He's an asshole and fucked with her one too many times. I think he provoked her. He beat on her, neglected her, and used sex as a weapon. You know? All that whole time he was selling me baking soda?!"

"WHAAA!" I said, trying to maintain a straight face.

"I don't agree with what she did, but I understand." Benjamin continued.

"And leaving him was never an option?"

"She always had an excuse. She wanted to leave but didn't. I don't know, she sounded—"

"Conflicted?"

"Yeah! Like whatever decision she made, it would be a bad one."

October 2019

I flip-flopped careers. I worked in customer service since I "retired from hair." I finally received a job offer with Public Service Enterprise Group (PSE&G)- I answered customer calls and complaints for New Jersey's largest provider of electric and natural gas services, so my schedule changed. I hung out less but knew nothing had changed, except I stopped buying the E&J and cigarettes. Shortly after, Benjamin downgraded liquors to VSOP—same great taste, cheaper, bigger bottle. Daisy showed up more in the fall. She donned the latest Burberry hoodie, kept her hair pale blonde, and always wore purple Beats. I couldn't quite tell if she was mixed or just very light-skinned.

When she came, she unfortunately didn't know when to leave. Benjamin and I only hung out one or two nights a week now. She was being a real block-buster. (Block-buster: a person who stops the sex from happening.) She was cool enough, though. Daisy worked as a chef at a posh steakhouse in Alpine. Her vibe was different, and she outwardly did not have a taste for Tabitha. They would sit quietly next to each other but, one at a time, chew Ben's ear off. Daisy wasn't a big fan of cocaine, so that meant she wasn't fond of Karim, either.

We wore jackets and hoodies to smoke outside as the weather chilled. When it rained, we would huddle under the summer shade umbrella, which stayed open all year. Friends would come and go, but in the fall, it became the five, sometimes six of us. Benny and me, Karim, Tabitha, Keith, and sometimes Daisy. The gossip about Keith was he didn't work and lived with his mother; he and Karim were brothers with the same father. Keith leached off of Karim for drugs and alcohol. That's why they were always around. Since Ben let them smoke and drink, they made his backyard their nighttime hangout.

In between laughs, pulls, and bullshit stories, Karim would be seen snorting into his sleeve. One time, I asked, "How much for a bump?"

"Oh! You wanna try white girl?"

"Huh—"

"White girl, you know, she my lil' white girl. You wanna try?"

"Yea-how much?"

"Five dollars."

I looked at Ben and asked, "You wanna try it?"

"Yeah!"

"Give me twenty dollars."

"'Kay..."

"Here!" I handed Karim the twenty Benjamin gave me. He chopped it up with his driver's license and sectioned off four lines of cocaine on the one-sided CD case. As he handed it to me, with the white-and-red-striped cut straw, I smiled in his direction as he said, "Be careful. This shit will fuck you up." Ben and I looked at each other and nodded as we silently agreed that's what we wanted. Since Daisy was uncomfortable around it, we decided to code-word it "Britney Spears" instead of "white girl." Karim winked and said, "So we don't racially divide."

The rush of adrenaline, the pull of gravity. I felt heavy. Walking would be a challenge.

It was immobilizing at first, with a tinge of devil-may-care. It was funny, whatever "it" was at the moment. I understood Beavis and Butthead much better. I said what I felt and had no shame—it was liberating. I told a story, and everybody laughed like a sitcom. I wanted more of it because I could feel it wear off, and before I knew it, I was slapping down a twenty from my pocket. Once the third blunt was lit, I needed water. Instead, I downed the rest of the E&J soda mix. That night, sex with Benjamin was more enjoyable and very slippery.

Benjamin

Hey! What are you doing

4:17pm

Nothing. Why do you ask?

Nick just came through with a
new batch. Girl Scout Cookies
...wanted to know if you
wanted to smoke

4:45pm

Nah actually, I just
smoked and I'm good

Alrighty then next time

As soon as I saw the caller ID, I assumed he knew. Karim must've told him. I'm a horrible liar, so I didn't want to get into a conversation or even go see him.

April 11th, 3:30 AM

I took Karim back to my place the night of the initial text, knowing my boys were asleep. After he looked around, he agreed it was a nice spot. He got comfortable. His clothes came off in a pile by the chair. He left his socks on and smiled as he crawled into bed. I was still half-dressed, wanting him to watch me remove my clothes. In the bed, he fell sweetly into my arms. I felt love with his kisses and instantly wanted more. He warmed my skin with his flesh. He lay on top of me as he tangled his legs around me. I could feel his girth between my thighs. I relaxed under his weight. I was surprised by his mouth as it touched my body everywhere. I suddenly gasped for air and giggled at the way he explored me. I jumped at the spread of his tongue compared to the tip. I wanted him.

I remember him pulling me closer as he leaned back. He controlled me, centered me, and approached me from behind. I fell into it—it felt like a groove. I sensed his energy and excitement. I jerked forward. My shoulders dropped to the bed. I was pinned. I smiled at the nonverbal commands and made note of his confidence. He dominated, and I allowed it. His thrust met my gush as I prepared for his density and all of his length.

Treetops, mountains with waterfalls, and city skylines. I was flying. Clouds surrounded me. I closed my eyes to imagine floating, drifting, and sailing midair. I was hang-gliding over a picturesque day, slowly descending with each electrical charge that radiated throughout my body. I could hear myself in the distance: breathing, but more gasping for air. His electrical charges became me. He was two millimeters smaller than Ben, but he had him in performance and creativity. He twisted my body and met me on the side. I was dangling at one point. I asked for water and seconds once he was satisfied. I instantly melted from the inside. After seconds, I salivated for thirds. I slowly ascended to earth, safely to my bed. I needed his schedule for the next couple of weeks, with holidays and weekends included.

Karim cuddled up and appeared comfortable in my house, in my bed, in me. I could hear my mother talking about trifling men who need a place to stay. I heard myself talk over her to tell him he didn't need to leave.

He encompassed everything I could love and more: young, dangerous, intimidating, aggressive, articulate, brazen, alpha, gainfully employed, AND handsome? I would never find this combination again.

Maybe I could be his girlfriend or at least a secret lover? Impossible. I could never allow myself to revere him, and he agreed. So, for now, I allowed my life's mantra to lead the way: Just Have Fun!

For how long? Was there an extended warranty, or do you have to take it as-is?

CHAPTER THREE

Fall of 2019

Benjamin and Tabitha worked the same schedule at the same supermarket. They talked every night. After I won the city's lottery for an income-based luxury three bedroom/two bath apartment their behaviors started to change in weird ways. When I texted her to help me move; she didn't answer back. Two days later, I asked for pills. She texted right away. I remember the look on her face when she congratulated me. Part smile, part hover-face. (Hover-face: when you have a completely different facial expression waiting for your smile to fade. Like when Ivanka Trump walked in front of Melaina at the White House podium.)

I noticed a change in Ben's communication when she was around. It was like he was recalling their behind-my-back conversations and forgetting I hadn't been there.

One Thursday night, it was raining, so Tabitha, Benjamin, and I smoked in the Jeep. He abruptly spoke, "Oh! You gotta be careful of DYFS!"

I looked puzzled. "Department of Youth and Family Services?" I questioned.

"Yes!"

"Whaaa?"

"I told Tabitha about what happened with your sons and Tabitha said since the high school called you about your sons smoking weed in the bathroom, they might call DYFS too because they're both underage and you could lose your apartment."

"WHAAA?!" My head paused in his direction, and I squinted my eyes.

"It's true," Tabitha chimed in. "They did the same thing to my mother when my sister got arrested for smoking weed underage. She lost her apartment!"

"You gotta be careful," Benjamin repeated. "You could lose your apartment."

"Don't say no dumb shit like that to me!"

"Well, you could." She was sure.

"You sound stupid! He didn't get arrested. It was his first offense. They're not even pressin' char—matter of fact, we not even talkin' 'bout this no more. Y'all don't know what the fuck ya talkin' 'bout."

I heard some rustlings and sighs, but neither of them said anything else. I remember searching between their faces with the look of go-ahead-and-say-something-else. I rolled my eyes and talked about the rain letting up and how we should make our way back inside.

I tired of Tab's attitude, and she made being around her uncomfortable. Her intentions were to downplay me. So, I in turn intentionally said things to completely agitate her. One night in our backyard smoke sessions, Karim got a call, got up and yelled, "Coming right back." He said it often but rarely did. That night, he came back a few hours later. As he approached, Tabitha was talking about him, and when he heard her, he stood silently to eavesdrop. I was the only one who saw him. I shook my head, he motioned to me to be quiet. I had a wide grin because she faced me.

She continued, "He's always at my job..." and moved closer to the table. Looked over the wrong shoulder and whispered. "I saw him watching me from outside the store." Her demeanor spoke fear of him. She was convinced he was stalking her from the parking lot. Since she was a cashier and stood in front of huge pane windows.

Karim cracked his bottle open; she snapped her head to the right and saw him there within earshot. She looked back at me with a glance of pure detest. I puckered, I'm sure.

According to Tab, Ben and her were best buddies. "Ben," she said, "is the boys' godfather, and since you're dating him, you're their godmother."

"Ah! Noo." I heard myself say.

Benjamin enjoyed their time together and shrugged it off as he was giving her free therapy sessions.

"With what degree?" I once asked him.

He straight-up believed, allowing her to talk without question or debate, "she would hear herself." The only problem with that theory is that she always thought she was right.

Since he didn't have a college degree in Psychology or any experience with a therapist, I warned him, "This is dangerous to get involved in. Both her and Karim have real mental issues and need real guidance and sound advice, maybe medication."

"Eh! I don't have anything else to do" was his excuse for meddling and gossiping with this unstable girl. The same excuse I would use if someone caught me watching Keeping Up With the Kardashians. If Karim and Tabitha were a reality show, Benjamin was the street Dr. Phil.

The more time he allowed her to tell her untruths, broken narratives, and brandish brash arrogance; the more time she had to plot. Little things she would say about Karim when he wasn't around allowed me to know she secretly hated him.

I would often ask, "Why don't you just leave him?"

Every time, there was a different answer. But one of the last times, she said, "I am."

"OH! You have a plan?"

"Yes. I have to move. There's no way I could live here and not see him."

"Where you going?"

"Queens. I'm going to stay with my Aunt Shareece in Queens until I can get my place."

"Oh, wow! This is a big decision. When are you leaving?"

"Next week. I need some time to pack my things and get the boys' papers."

"AWW, babe...we gotta have a backyard smash before she leaves."

Benjamin looked up from his tablet and nodded.

A few weeks later, I noticed she was still around, and their relationship

43

became even more vindictive. Ben knew he took on more than he could when Tabitha told him Karim beat her. I was livid at the abuse and her excuses to stay. I didn't understand the acceptance of it in your life or around your children. She talked of the abuse as if he were always the aggressor and she had no choice but to stay around and accept it. She excused his behavior because she said, "he always looks out for me."

Even financial help doesn't allow a man, or woman, the right to put their hands on you. I had my fair share of domestic violence and didn't want to hear someone close to me going through it. I was numb. I thought real quick she could also be wanting to vilify him since she knew my interest and saw our chemistry. Was she playing victim?

Tuesday night, Benjamin and I planned to have dinner, smoke, let a movie play, and have sex. He asked me if we could hang out with her instead.

"She's having a hard time and needs a shoulder."

"About what…?"

"I'll make it up to you and promise she won't be long—thirty-five minutes!"

He shouldn't have said that, because the minute I saw her, I started my mental stopwatch. After our initial cordialities and setting up the drinks, I started in, "Hey! What's going on?" I wanted her to spill the beans and explain what was so pressing she needed to talk to him tonight.

"Oh nothing, just need to talk to Ben about the job and how they trying to fire me."

No, that wasn't it, but this was some gossip I hadn't heard before. She started from the beginning how they didn't like her taking so many breaks. Then her story looped back around to Karim stalking her and having to leave her post to tell him to go home.

I exploded, "You're losing your job because of Karim?"

"Yeah! He's out there after he gets off work—sometimes for 40 minutes!"

"He comes to pick you up, no?"

"Yeah, but why is he out there for so long?"

"What does he say?"

"He's taking a nap or rolling up to smoke…"

"And…?"

"And waiting on me."

"So, it's not stalking. It's waiting…I thought you said you were leaving?"

"I am! I just have to get some things together and make sure the boys' doctor and school records are in order."

"What?!" I pretended I couldn't hear her.

"I have to enroll them in a new school. And get their vaccines and stuff."

"Well, Benjamin told me about him hurting you. I'm sorry you're going through this, but you have to leave to protect you and your boys. I know it's not gonna be easy. I left my father with my mother when I was little, and I left with my two boys, so I know it's not easy, but in the long run, you'll be happier. You seem miserable now. You have to leave him."

"I am." The second time she lied to my face.

"Both of y'all are crazy. Somebody's bound to get hurt or even worse." I squinted to see if she heard me.

It was a difficult conversation, but after thirty-three minutes, she had to get going. So, I suggested she go home, get some rest, and think about what I had said. I was hungry and horny, and she had already destroyed the first half an hour. I couldn't allow her to linger around and fuck up the rest of the night. She had to go, and I'm glad she was willing 'cause who knows what part of the Bronx would've come out.

After that exchange, she staged a coup. Her main objective was to put a wedge in my relationship with Ben. She wouldn't see me or talk to me after that night. He sided with her and said I had been rude and dismissive

45

of her feelings. *"She came to talk to me; you took over and told her to leave."* He said I needed to apologize to her. I scoffed at the idea because her mental illness wouldn't accept my apology, even if it was sincere.

But I took his advice to make amends. I texted:

Even though she told Benjamin that she would never forgive me. I thought this was the most childish thing I had ever been involved in and wanted nothing but safety for her and her children. She concluded I just apologized because Ben made me, which was true, and now we enjoyed nights together alone, except he sulked and was elusive. I defended my position, but he never forgave me for putting his friend on the stand like that and making her feel as if she had to leave his house because of me.

"I'm sorry. I said I was sorry. What else do you want me to do?"

"Nothing."

Our relationship was never the same.

April 16th, 2020

We were still living in the pandemic. Social distancing, masks, and gloves to go into stores and restaurants— Karim was coming over the next day. This was a story to be sold. I'm thinking...how?

Okay, listen—Young Crazy Love Triangle. Tabitha and the two brothers, but, all the while, she's secretly in love with Benjamin because he listens. She thinks the love with Karim is real because they started young, and he is all she knows: financially supportive, the bomb, rough sex, free drugs, and booze. Except she loves talking and cannot communicate with Karim as freely as she does with Benjamin. She has verbal diarrhea, and he seems to care; he's a safe place for her and the kids. Karim's "love" is scrappy and loud, sometimes pushy, and stalker-ish, but always intoxicating. He's a real bad boy and she can't get enough. Rob Stone's beat drops for "Chill Bill."

I come in pretty and flirty. She sees me as a threat on both sides. Her best friend and her man. They talk so much she convinces Benjamin I'm to blame for suggesting she leave Karim. She defames me by insinuating I want her on again/off again lover of eight years. She would rather kill him and end up in prison for 10-20 than walk away from his toxic, juicy, abusive drug.

He pushes that same drug on me, flirting since day one, and now, as Tabitha is taken away in handcuffs in front of her grandmother's house, kids crying, silver Mercedes out front, and her head held at shame level, we can be seen passionately kissing in the Jeep across the street. We suddenly drop out of camera view. Fade to black.

For the first month, we saw each other weekly. Karim was always off the cuff, very candid. I appreciated the truth he told with no apology. I was one of two. Well, actually, I was number two since Tab left. I met him Saturday night at his house. He was already out front. We sat in his car and played music. He liked old school R&B and started to sing along with the chorus to "Forever my Lady" by Jodeci. It was funny to watch because it softened his character, and I saw him playful for the first time. Soon after the song finished, I told him I preferred the current trap music with Jersey club. I wanted him to play "Sasuke" by Lil Uzi Vert. He said he never heard it. I shook my head, what is this generation coming to?

He was charming, he was sweet, he was attentive, he was engaging, and he was well-endowed. He also enjoyed cuddling. I wondered if Tabitha just brought out the worst in him. Now, he was completely relaxed and thanked her for getting locked up to allow him peace. He had money to spend differently and appreciated her far away. He said she was the toxic one. He spoke openly about their relationship, meeting in high school and dating at seventeen. After high school she got married and she cheated on her husband with him. That's why they both think the youngest boy is his. They do favor with the same spicy mustard complexion.

I pressed again on "that night" she shot his brother as he lit the blunt.

"She crazy!" And paused with the look of 'that's it'. "That's why she was always calling me to know where I was every minute— because she at home, fuckin'."

"I'm sure something out of the ordinary happened to make her put her gun in the car and drive to see you."

"She crazy!" He said, coughing and passing the blunt.

"You said you had plans that night, yes?"

"Yeah! And she over at Ben's house, probably fuckin' him!"

"When was the last time you saw her before that night?"

"Oh! We had a good time at my boy's crib. Him and his lady was there, and we was havin' a good ole time..."

He smiled as he recalled Sunday night when they snorted, smoked weed, drank hard liquor, and dropped acid.

"Had she done that before?"

"Nah, I don't think so..."

"She was trippin.' That shit don't wear off next day!"

"Yea—"

"It was good for you?"

"Yea man, we was good. We spent the night and left the next day. She called me, but I didn't see her again until she got out the car with the gun."

"She aimed it?"

"No. It was in her hand tho—"

We finished smoking and went back to my house. With a lapse in judgment, I wanted him to Netflix and chill with me. He would have to meet my teenage sons. Thai, 16, and Cue, 17.

Before the end of the month people were getting restless at home and demanded the restrictions to be lifted. Quarantine had raged some, not being able to get haircuts became an issue. Protests erupted over extended mask use and not being able to return to work are real sticking points for people around the country.

"Several states protest the COVID-19 "lockdowns" or "stay-at-home" rules issued by their governors. They view lockdowns and stay-at-home rules as infringements on their personal liberty. They carry signs such as "Don't Tread on Me", "Give Me Liberty or Give Me Death", and "Open Our Bars". At the Michigan protest, people chanted "Open Up Michigan!" And "Lock Her Up" (speaking of Michigan Governor Gretchen Whitmer). Some protests yelled about wanting haircuts." With their hair so long, they needed headbands. "At least a dozen barbers turned up to cut hair at a rally at the Michigan Capitol. US President Donald Trump encouraged their protests by tweeting:

"LIBERATE MINNESOTA!", "LIBERATE MICHIGAN!", and "LIBERATE VIRGINIA!"

Brad J. Bushman Ph. D (2020, April 21) You Want to Get a Haircut? I Want to Not Die of COVID-19, Psychology Today

I recall one news clip where some were holding signs that simply read, "I NEED A HAIRCUT!" I scoffed at the ignorance of the privileged.

CHAPTER FOUR

May 9th, 2020

    Little Richard, King of Rock, and Roll is no longer with us. (8)

May 25th

    America watches George Floyd slowly diminish under the knee of Derek Chauvin. Black Americans are outraged, more so by the nonchalant stare in the eyes of "the officer/overseer." The video shows no resistance of arrest, maybe a question of arrest, but definitely not throw-you-on-the-ground and put-a-knee-in-your-neck-for-nine-and-a-half-minutes resist of arrest.

    Americans everywhere, or those who value Black lives, are determined to be heard. This "overseer" has to be held accountable. Daily protests erupt in major cities. Small towns hold rallies and protests. Unfortunately, also followed by looters, disorderly conduct, and tear gas. Large groups formed daily at the same time mass people are out of work it became The Year of 2020- Go protest. Those who had had just about enough of the "justice" system. And how it works for the selected few but definitely not for "We, the people." Police are given the right to kill without question and overseers routinely kill unarmed black people. (Black men are three and a half times more likely to be shot and killed by a police officer than white men in America.) (9)

    It seems like innocent people are dying at the hands of law enforcement and all the politicians want are the riots and the looting to stop. No bother the Black lives lost. America: not the safest place to be Black. We have to educate ourselves and our children in the law. Our job as parents, Black parents, is to instill peace and self-acceptance. Groups of Blacks are moving to Japan, Tokyo, and Hong Kong. I'm a traitor if I want change. Good riddance if I leave and if you stay, shut the fuck up and take what we give you, boy.

June 6th

    Dave Chappelle does the first socially distanced "comedy" show entitled "8:46."

June 14th

News kept close coverage on the protests, and social media insisted they were all peaceful demonstrations. My small town participated in the marches and my Instagram feed kept me involved. I felt the need to push past the fear of COVID-19 and join my local brethren for police reform. On Saturday morning, I got up early and found where my neighbors had already started the rally. The streets were barricaded, and it felt like hundreds walked to the beat of the loudspeaker's chants and jeers. There were all shades of color in attendance, which I enjoyed the most.

At first, the high schoolers led with spoken word and cries for us to look into the future. Their voices were eerily familiar, and some brought up valid points of unity is strength. Three public officials vowed for real change; the crowd cheered the town's mayor as he recognized our pain and asked for continued peace. We walked under an hour up Cedar Lane and around the corner which brought us to the courthouse and city hall. Many had signs that read, "JUSTICE FOR GEORGE," "DON'T SHOOT." Many more read, "BLACK LIVES MATTER."

June 15th

My Instagram crush led a march in the adjacent town with a bullhorn. Even though I had just attended my own march yesterday, his organized march seemed better on Instagram. In his video, the viewer sees him from the front, black hat, yellow shirt with a fist. He stops, calls out, and proceeds again as his friend with the camera lets the crowd walk by. Seeing the variety of shapes, colors, and sizes, and how far back he was heard was impressive. When my IG crush called, "What do we want?" the assembly behind him answered, "JUSTICE!"

He continued, "When do we want it?

NOW!

What do we want?

JUSTICE!

When do we want it?

NOW!

What do we want?

JUSTICE

When do we want it?

NOW!

And if we DON'T get it?

SHUT IT DOWN!

If we DON'T get it?

SHUT IT DOWN!

If we DON'T get it?

SHUT IT DOWN!

And if we DON'T get it?

SHUT IT DOWN!

HANDS UP

DON'T SHOOT!

HANDS UP

DON'T SHOOT!

HANDS UP!

DON'T SHOOT!

HANDS UP!

DON'T SHOOT!

Say HIS NAME!

GEORGE FLOYD

Say HIS NAME!

TAMIR RICE

Say HIS NAME!

PHILANDO CASTILE

Say HIS NAME!

                               ERIC GARNER

Say HER NAME

                               BREONNA TAYLOR

Say HER NAME

                               SANDRA BLAND

Say HER NAME

                               ATATIANA JEFFERSON

Say HER NAME

                               TANISHA ANDERSON

WHAT DO WE WANT?

                               JUSTICE!

AND. If. We. DON'T. GET IT?!

                               SHUT. IT. DOWN!"

Next thing I knew, I wanted to sing the chant with a crazy dope beat. I thought of him often. Strong, fearless, so domineering at five foot four and 150 pounds soaking wet, with his beautiful brown skin, full beard, and intense eyes.

June 18th, 2015

I remember the piercing stare he gave me at an upper Manhattan nightclub. It was my LaGuardia High School girlfriend's birthday party. We went to the same high school, but we met only after Facebook "re"united us. I enjoyed her energy and fierceness. Funny as it was, she was the ugly duckling from freshman to junior year. N'neka (Class of '91) became a successful music mogul and a take-your-breath-away stunner. She was five foot two with smooth mocha skin, a zero-inch waist, and a down-her-back (you couldn't tell if it was her real hair, very expensive) wavy weave.

N'neka commanded the room with her presence. It's a combination of grown woman swag and divine goddess energy. The dress suction-cupped her body with ease. Flutes of champagne glasses were handed to her on demand as she offered me one. I stood in her spotlight for a second and felt the eyes of men jousting for her attention.

Haphazardly enough, she introduced me to him. When I asked her, "Which one is your man?"

She laughed and said, "Not-a-one...but which one would I take home? It would be..." She looked around and hummed while scanning what felt like the entire room. Then, she pointed. "Him!"

His eyes followed her finger and knew on demand to stand up and cross the dance floor. I was in amazement. He leaned in and whispered in her ear. He read African with bright white teeth, precision beard, and exquisite taste. I could just tell from the gold silk bomber jacket, tailored pants, and loafers with no socks. They conversed for a minute, they laughed. I felt odd standing there, thought, maybe I should go sit down. Just as soon as I turned to walk away, she grabbed my arm and whispered, "He says he knows you."

"Whaaa?" Sheer confusion and dismay covered my face. I could tell he'd already looked me from head to toe and I hadn't even gotten a good look at his face, I mean, rich dark melanated skin, nice teeth, beard and dazzling eyes...didn't ring a bell. I knew I had never met this beautiful man before. She pivoted between us once more, came back, and said, "You live in Jersey, don't you?"

Puzzled, I shook my head and said, "Yea—"

I do hair—we're pretty good with faces, but I still couldn't recall meeting him. N'neka and Chocolate Brown Bliss switched places. He leaned in and said, "I own the barber shop on Westfield Drive. The Gentlemen's Barber."

He smelled of honeycombs and burnt vanilla. I could hear him and understood every word he spoke, but I had a look of wonder and disbelief. My heart rate was over the resting level just standing there.

He introduced himself officially that night, and as we spoke, I'm sure I laughed and quoted my credentials. I don't remember what cloud I was on. He appeared surprised when he realized I didn't just "do hair" but also *taught cosmetology. We pulled out our phones, texted each other and locked numbers in. When I realized, the banter was coming to an end, I leaned in further and said, "You have to tell me—what are you wearing?" His cologne was all I wanted around me.*

"Tom Ford." I heard him say with a smile.

I took one more deep inhale and promised to speak soon.

N'neka's party was a smash. There was a moment when the DJ slipped up for close to 90 seconds and there was no music. Someone in the crowd shouted, "NO MUSIC?!" Four beats later the dance floor erupted. "NO MUSIC! (clap-clap/clap-clap) NO MUSIC! (clap-clap/clap-clap) NO MUSIC! (clap-clap/clap clap) NO MUSIC!" It was great. We filled the space with laughter and fun and allowed the DJ a minute to bring the beat back. We partied till the club closed at 3am. Filtering outside, everyone looked different in the streetlights: overly happy, a lil' intoxicated, and maybe even a little frisky.

I just wanted N'neka to know I knew how to hang. As we hugged, I told her to keep enjoying her nights, days, and years to come. I looked around and the African was standing there—I assumed to escort her to the after-party. I waved in his direction and walked back to the car, headed for Jersey.

I stopped a few minutes later to get a plate from the Caribbean spot on 127th Street. While getting my curry goat, rice, and peas, I ran into another LAG alum: Dre. He approached me first and thank goodness he did—I would've never picked him out of a line-up. I had to go back to Facebook just to remember his name.

As soon as I pulled onto my block, I got a call from the African. He asked if I was still in the area, could he get a ride back to Jersey?

"Awww, I'm already home," I replied. I smiled all the way inside. That would've been a stimulating night.

After that, I followed him on Instagram. Insta-love. Insta-infatuation. Insta-crush. I never called him, and he never followed me back. But I got a front-row seat into his life. I watched him travel, eat gourmet food, bask in Africa's sun with the look of peace and content. I watched him riding camels and taking pics in front of breathtaking monuments for five straight years. I lived in quiet envy of his apparently abundant life. I sat at home, worked overtime and double tapped on IG.

June 12th

BAP (Black And Proud) *Instagram @jessieB803*

My hair is my Heritage. White girls pay for my melanin.

My lips, my clothes, my swag, my coat. They all want to get what I got by the white folk. But no, not no mo'. This generation said hell no. If you don't love love and you hate for fun. Hit the road, Jack, you gotta go.

I'M BLACK AND I'M PROUD. Let me say it loud. I'M BLACK AND I'M PROUD. I love the style. I'M BLACK AND I'M PROUD. I'ma move the crowd. I'M BLACK AND I'M PROUD. Let the world hear the song.

I'M BLACK AND I'M PROUD. I'M BLACK AND I'M PROUD.

I'M BLACK AND I'M PROUD. I'M BLACK AND I'M PROUD.

Pecan tan, black like sand this melanin can't come in a can.

This Jack fella here better cut the check, get his face painted black like Malcolm X. But no, not no mo', Kim K got a booty like the globe.

Inject they lips, inject they hips, having you praying to the lord- you look like this. Hell no! I say hell no. Love the skin you in baby, glow!

No matter the skin you been born with, put that lotion on, give the world a show!

Pick up your skin. Just smile and grin. No matter what your color, better love your skin. And no, I'm not a racist, I'm just stating facts,

I see a lot of white girls wish they had it like this. Black!

I'M BLACK AND I'M PROUD. Let me say it loud. I'M BLACK AND I'M PROUD. I love the style. I'M BLACK AND I'M PROUD. I'ma move the crowd. I'M BLACK AND I'M PROUD. Let the world hear the song.

I'M BLACK AND I'M PROUD. I'M BLACK AND I'M PROUD.

I'M BLACK AND I'M PROUD. I'M BLACK AND I'M PROUD. Bye.

June 2020

Louisville passes "Breonna's Law," which bans "No-Knock" warrants and requires officers to wear body cameras when carrying out search warrants. The Louisville police chief was fired after it came to light officers involved in the fatal shooting were not wearing body cameras during the raid. (8)

June 18th, 2020

Karim had been to the house a few times, and this time the boys and I smoked with him outside on the top floor of the parking garage. Karim and Thai hit it off and were sitting in his car while Cue and I were standing in front. We were standing in silence, when suddenly Cue said he didn't like the way Karim was looking at him. I was confused because the sheer glare of the sun wouldn't have given a clear view anyway. We were all high. I made light of it, trying to diminish any feelings of ill will. I should've remembered what Cue had said earlier: "Ma— I don't like this dude." I was sure free weed would set his mind at ease.

I said, "What? You're crazy!", "He said it again but this time louder, "I don't like the way he's looking at me!" Now I'm looking at Karim for some hint at what's going on. He smiles.

Cue all of a sudden rages and calls him a fraud and a loser. Karim gets up out of the car, looks at me and then back at Cue. I understood his confusion. I was between them and tried to look Cue in the eye, but he had gone somewhere else—it was like I didn't know him. The last thing I remember is Cue yelling, "DO ME A FAVOR and STAY THE FUCK OUTTA WESTFIELD! FUCKIN' PUNK, FUCKIN' LOSER!"

That's when I yelled, "CUE! GET IN THE HOUSE!" I looked for Thai to go with him.

Karim said he had to go. I couldn't blame him. When he said he couldn't come back, I held back tears. This did not just happen. He said, "I can't fight a teenager. I'm a grown man. I'll be put in jail first and last to come home.

I could lose my job. I can't handle any more drama."

I was devastated. I was the drama!?

Couple weeks later, I saw him again at his grandmother's house, in his room. I couldn't get over being in Nana's house with his socks and dirty laundry. There was no way I could be caught in his room by his uncle or one of his aunties. If I stepped out of that room and looked my age group in the eye, I would be extremely embarrassed—and then it dawned on me: he's eight years older than my son. Right then, I understood how Cue felt: disrespected in his own home where he finds comfort and peace.

When I got home, I finally asked Cue what had bothered him so much that he cursed the man out and damned him from Westfield.

"You don't know?"

I shook my head.

"You don't know what he asked my little brother?"

With wide eyes, I remained silent.

"That motherfucker asked him how long it would take him to move an ounce."

With a heavy heart, I agreed with his reaction and thanked him for his diligence.

We had to cut ties. I just stopped calling, but Karim blocked me. I only realized it after a month of not talking. He texted me and asked for a haircut. I would've been honored. But when I texted him to confirm the time, I got no response. I tried calling, leaving messages to no avail. My heart was broken from our two-month love affair. I would lie awake at night and masturbate with thoughts of my baby buddy's long stroke game. Damn, I missed him.

July 1st

My sexual wants and desires ran hard during COVID. I resorted back to my old ways of finding dick on the internet. My personal favorite site never let me down. Well, almost never. For someone who doesn't have space or time for a serious relationship, I do a casual. It suits me better to know *they have a place to go when we're finished. I want someone not looking to stay or shack up in my place. A married man, preferably. Even though I don't explicitly say that in my bio, at least these people understand they are "going home" after.*

For six weeks. I'd had no sex. So, browsing through spread eagle photos, dick pics, and fucking videos was touching on my warm spots. As soon as I reactivated my account, I got dozens of hits from dozens of men: old, young, White, Black, and Puerto Rican. No Asian men, even though they turn me on the most. By day three, I whittled down my options to the top five. I sent messages, started talking, flirting, showing way too much skin, and receiving things most people would call pornographic. Except I don't do the nudes, and, oddly enough, I feel violated by unsolicited pictures of the male genitalia. How can someone have a conversation with a dick?

Day four, I got seven new messages. One was from a "Mr. Perfect," and it said, "SHHHH! Don't say anything. Just get in your car and come over tonight."

Mr. Perfect was the African I met at N'neka's party, my Insta-crush, the man with the perfect beard and teeth, and smelling like Tom Ford and owning his own business in my neighborhood for the last 12 years. The message intrigued me. I read it over and over again. Six times to be exact with my mouth open. I forget to breathe, and I remember putting my head down. I had to remember to think, more or less, respond. How can I say, "OKay!" without seeming too anxious? I wanted to respond with the right tone and the appearance of sophistication.

But I couldn't get out of my head—if he was dating and attracted to N'neka, how could he be attracted to me? We have very different body types, opposite skin tones, and acute styles. I had to lay down to process this new information.

I slept the whole night and jumped up the next morning with him on my mind. I had to respond. Still in bed, I wrote back, "Is the invite still open?" I waited. Feeling silly, I went about my day not expecting a response until the evening. But when I went back to check a few hours later, he said,

Mr. Perfect

You coming?

> Do you remember me?

From Walgreens?

> No, we met a few years
> ago at N'neka's party

At The Corner Spot, right?

> I think so

Oh yeah! You gave me a
ride home that night?

> No, but yeah, we
> met that night

Oh, my bad! So you
coming or what?

> Yeah! But I don't want
> you to see me just as a
> sexual deviant. I want to
> be a business partner
> and a travel companion.

There was a long pause as if he stepped away from the computer.

My gut told me to put it all on the line; if he accepted, I would be appreciated for more than just sex. My last sex partner was amazing, and I fell in love with him just because of his interests and worldviews. But when I told him I liked him, he backed away faster than a cornered jackal. I was insulted and demoralized. I wanted more and promised myself the next man I met on the sex line would know me and not just my kitty cat.

After a few hours, he responded,

This is a sex site, not LinkedIn. You sound like you got a contract for me to sign. If that were to happen, don't you think it should happen organically?

I was flabbergasted. I was shot down and had no comeback. I deleted the messages, closed my computer, and went on with my day, life, and search for new penis. I was just astonished by the way he spoke and shut me down. But what did I expect? An open invitation to his next business meeting and round-trip tickets? Maybe I played it all wrong...DAMN! I fucked it up.

July 6th-13th

TIME magazine's cover is a silhouette of a Black girl with braids pulled into a top bun. Inside her hair, a bubble of fire with protesters, a man with a long gun, and people's fists. The girl's shoulders are a boutique of dripping red and pink roses. The background and foreground blend well to show two distinct stories. The bottom half of the girl's face is covered in gray stars with a light blue back. The top half is gray behind her with white vertical stripes fading at her temples. It appears at first to be stars and stripes but could also symbolize bars. I see a strong young woman, maybe ready to shed a tear. I see America divided in half with her stuck in the middle. One half is ready to ignite her right to protest and possibly put her behind bars, with the lower half a cool blue embroidered with roses of remembrance and love. The bleeding symbolizes our internal pain. The cover is entitled "America Must Change."

July 18th

United States Representative John Lewis, a civil rights pioneer, dies of cancer at eighty. He wrote, in his memoir Across that Bridge: A Vision for Change and A Future for America, "You are a light. You are light. Never let anyone—any person or any force—dampen, dim, or diminish your light." (10)

July 27th

Simone Biles, the greatest gymnast of all time, steps down from the Tokyo Olympics, "I have to focus on my mental health." (11)

August 7th

Cardi B and Megan Thee Stallion's WAP music video premieres to mixed reviews.

MrPerfect

11:49pm

Whats up

Hi

Wanna play? Don't be shy and over-think, let's just have a good time. Reading your profile let's me know ur a freak just like me let me indulge

My apologies. I feel like shit... I will have to catch you next weekend & play. I promise

Are u sick? I'm addicted to spontaneous play not planning

What are you afraid of? I like it nasty n messy let a king indulge in how he likes it I like super thick meat not some uptight nasty freak

We will meet, not scared. This week is a bad week I do like to play & be nasty be dominated so I look forward to it & especially with you, king

MrPerfect

11:49pm

I'm horny let's fuck

Don't wanna fuck someone new

I'm bleeding

It's always something with you How long? A full 7 days?

LOL
Yes

What day is that? SMH

I thought you said you liked it messy

Yes come over and get cream-pied

What's the address

Give me a sec babe. We should go to a sex club tonight as well. Wait no not on your red lol i live at the Excalibur on Prospect

MrPerfect

oh ok...what's your number

Call me I want to hear your voice before I leave

Calling in 5

He called in fifteen and, instantly, I was transported back to the close talk we had that night on the dance floor. His tone and timber bathed over my skin as he told me, *"Most women come over and see how I live and ask way too many questions. Imagine if I were a street thug who lived with his mother—you wouldn't ask him questions like, why do you love me or why choose me? You wouldn't ask him why he loves you 'cause you already would know why. 'Cause you're taking care of him. So, because I don't need you to care for me, you question me. Listen—I'm attracted to big girls because I get bored with skinny ones; they always sound like I'm hurting them. A big girl knows how to take it. So, come confident, don't ask so many questions because if I wasn't attracted to you, I wouldn't be inviting you up. And another thing—don't compliment me on my skin tone. It's the one thing I didn't have anything to do with and the only thing I can't do anything about. Find something else to compliment me on..."*

"Oh, okay—"

"I can tell you like extra kinky shit."

"Oh, really? What kinky shit I like?" "You liked to be fucked in the..."

(This portion of the conversation was omitted due to the graphic nature.)

65

"Well, come naked. I want to see your ass as soon as you walk through the door."

"Oh-kay—but doesn't your building have a doorman?"

"Oh, yes! So, you'll have to wear a coat."

"Okay, I just have to jump in the shower."

"How long will it take you to get here?"

"Clean or bushy?"

"How bushy?"

"A light Caesar."

"Okay hurry up!"

"'Kay...gimme thirty minutes."

I stopped to get a bottle to display proper manners. I remember being in awe of the incredible view of downtown Manhattan. His condo had all the amenities of a bachelor pad: wide screen television, a bar, zebra-skinned loveseat, ample seating, one-of-a-kind art pieces, and a massive fish tank. He asked me to come naked, so I wore only a bra and a tiny skirt with a trench. He complimented my fragrance with a hug—oils which I got in Harlem. He poured me a glass of CîROC, and we talked for a few minutes.

Then he made me wait while he showered. I can recall the night so vividly; I recorded the moment while waiting on the couch. I told myself to relish in it and take his advice to come confident, come strong, don't ask questions, and be sexy. The first video, I stressed his words to me, and in the second video, I said, "Be careful what you ask for. You just might get it." I panned the room then came back to me: happy face. Just then, I realized I didn't have any makeup on. Oh, My God! I didn't shit-shower-shave-makeup?! I didn't do it daily but always on dates. Well, since COVID I really hadn't been out, so he was lucky I shaved. I put down my phone and listened to the water still running. I was confused why it felt like the length of a sitcom since he'd gone in, it never took me this long to shower. Add on the time it took me to get there. it was my question to ask, "Why didn't you shower before, and why for so long?" I stormed into the bathroom at a minute past 43. I startled him, and he screamed. He had no shower curtain, so I saw it all before he grabbed his balls.

I thought it was funny and said, "What's taking so long?"

He yelled, "Get OUT!"

Once I had been there an hour, I started to notice the "leather" sectional was peeling, the fish tank had no fish—he most likely killed them. I didn't think it was a match. This man was a narcissist. (Narcissists have an extreme need for admiration, they also feel extreme entitlement and very little to no regard for others feelings and experiences. So, in love with themselves they genuinely are incapable of loving others.)

So, I'm on the couch, sulking, and he comes over and says, "Did you miss me?"

"What took so long?"

"I wanted to be fresh."

"Well...you do smell good."

"What do you know about Afrobeats?"

I shook my head. "Nothing..."

He rolled his eyes and seemed disappointed. I obviously had answered wrong and tried to correct myself. "...But I do know it's about time we get up on African music. It's awesome."

He agreed without speaking.

"Who's playing?"

"Wizkid..." We listened as he turned up the television playing videos. "Can I pour you some more?"

I was already feeling saucy. "Yes."

His sex was intense. In his lifestyle, BDSM is about control, pain, and humiliation. He insisted I stay with my head to the left, not looking at him. Any movement or giggling was seen as a violation; he would stop and say,

"You're acting. Do you want me to stop?"

"No"

"No, what—"

"No, Daddy."

"That's right and that's my name from now on, understand?"

"Yes—" He stopped and looked at me. "Yes, Daddy."

As soon as I complied with what he wanted, he bit my neck and my shoulder as he entered. His medium to average length had no girth and a little bit of a disappointment. He's thinner and shorter in person. His shoes must have had lifts. Then I noticed: It's not great when you're thinking of a man's footwear during sex. The African did have a rhythm and nice timing because we both climaxed together. He rolled over, exhausted. I looked and wondered if there would be a round two. It was nice, but I always appreciate more.

Throughout the night, I found out the rules and requirements of being a "Kept Woman" as told by my IG crush, The African, aka Mr. Perfect:

1) Have sex with anyone he chooses

2) Always stay dressed sexy and ready to get it in at any moment

3) Bring girls over

4) Clean and keep apartment tidy

5) When spending the night, rub his back with oils while he sleeps

6) Mild abuse: Must be open to scars from scratches, bites, and restraints

7) Frequent sex clubs

8) Change profile from single woman to couple

9) Never say no

10) Could be added as necessary

In my mind, I'm standing at the edge of the world, yelling, "I'm a 'Kept Woman?!' Wait! What was number four again?" I teetered on the thought *of having everything I wanted...but what boundaries had I set? I didn't sleep very well that night. My side of the bed enjoyed lower Manhattan's view, and I was captivated by the lights. I forgot to rub his back with the oils, even after giggling, I asked, "Well, where is it?" At one point during the night, I felt him stroke my back with two knuckles. I thought it sweet for a man I didn't think had the capacity to love others. It was endearing, nonetheless. I got up during the night to use the bathroom and look around.*

First, the shower curtain was missing because there was no rod, which was the oddest thing I'd seen. His rug was soaked and damp underneath my feet. I cringed the entire time I was sitting. I visited the kitchen and opened the fridge because, honestly, what else was there to do in a kitchen? It was packed with food delivery trays, water bottles, Tupperware, and a pan of cooked food not covered properly. A bag of lemons on the door was so molded, you could tell it'd been weeks since the last "Kept Woman" left. I quivered at the thought of going in there with a garbage can, Pine Sol/Fabuloso spray mix, Brillo pads and gloves. A face mask with a splash shield and chair. I took note of the amount of empty wine bottles on the counter and the sink full of glasses with a few dinner plates around the edge.

Number one and number four were out, and number three, getting girls to share with him? It would be like organizing a family reunion—too much work. So, I guess there was no deal. His proposition didn't even detail the benefits. What are the terms and conditions of this contract he is all too ready for me to sign?

As I made my way back to the window-side of the bed, I noticed the piles of clothes, hats, socks, and dirty towels tossed around the room. The seven-foot wooden carved giraffe standing in the corner of the immense bedroom was my favorite art piece. I couldn't sleep after I logged all of the dust, mold, and mildew up in there.

CHAPTER FIVE

1978

The year mommy had enough of the threats of abuse, being demeaned, belittled, and "punished" for not doing what she was told. Mental, physical, emotional, sexual, financial, and psychological abuse; she said she'd had enough, and we had to go. Uncle Leo, Fred, and Cousin Steve showed up one Saturday to pack a small U-Haul with our bunk bed, dressers, clothes, shoes, and toys. We left the toy chest and the mural Daddy painted. The last walk down the four flights of stairs is all I remember, crying and calling for Daddy to come too. I was five and confused. If mommy kissed me with tears in her eyes every night and said, "Go to sleep, baby. Everything will be okay in the morning," why wasn't it now?

Since that day, I was left craving a father figure to encourage and admire me for being me—to guide me and teach me how love is supposed to feel. To reassure me my body is sacred and tell me I am an Empress.

Touch being one of my love languages, I can feel love in a handshake, in a kiss, in between my legs, and in the weight of a man. I feel love during sex. I feel accepted, beautiful, and at ease—everything a girl feels when Daddy gives her his hand to cross the street. Daddy's hand was rough, but soft and powerful.

August 19th, 2020   *9:57PM*

August 28th, 2020

Chadwick "Black Panther/46/Thurgood Marshall/James Brown Forever"
Boseman loses his battle with cancer at the age of forty-four. (12)

September 10th   ***1:43PM***

"Hello?" I picked up on the first ring.

"Hey."

"Oh my God—long time—how are you?"

"I'm good..." my half-brother, Tarik, answered.

"Are you guys still in Atlanta?"

"Yea..."

"How are the—"

"Ahh..."

"—boys? How old are they now?"

"Yeah, they're great! Six and eight. But I called you—"

"Oh my God! What happened? What's going on?"

"I'm calling to tell you, Mark died today..."

"Oh—"

"Yeah, Grandma called me and told me he fell this morning coming down for breakfast."

"...was it Corona?"

"No. He had been sick, you know—" "Yeah, I know."

"—for several years with Diabetes."

"Yea, I know, so you're coming up?"

"Yes, I'll be there tomorrow."

"So, your wife and the kids are coming as well?"

"Yes, of course."

"It's horrible I get to meet them this way."

"Yea—"

"This is crazy. I just reached out to you on IG to get his number...I guess you're not on there much, huh?"

"No...I'm sorry. I'm just seeing your message now..."

"Wow..."

"Yea—"

"Soooo, what's Roberta's number?"

My grandmother was aghast. It sounded like tears at first and then pure shock.

Little did I know, she had caller ID and knew it was me before I said anything. I hadn't spoken to her in twenty years, so I understood her question, "Sunny...? How did you hear?"

I answered, "Tarik."

My half-brother and I met only once, fifteen years ago, with my half-sister, Zoe. My father, Mark, remarried and had a whole new family before I turned thirteen. I remember one of the last times he called me was to tell me baby Zoe was born. The next fourteen calls over the last thirty years were me calling him. The last call was a year ago, shortly after I returned from Belize. It was truly the best conversation I'd had with him. We shared scuba-diving stories and I found out things he had never told me. Like he, too, had visited Belize, trekked through New Zealand, and he went skydiving a few years before I went in 1999. He also told me he was writing a book.

My father chose not to be in my life.

The grandmother I knew as Roberta remained anonymous after the divorce. I broke the silence when I surprised everyone at her house for Thanksgiving dinner in 2000. Mark said he didn't want to share the visit with everyone else, so he didn't show up.

September 11th

May we never forget 9/11.

I awoke to the sound of broken glass and "SUNNY!" I jumped up and yelled "Yea?" I ran outside my room to the only man in my house, Cue, who was still sleeping. But he doesn't call me by my first name. I sat quietly, breathing, and listening to my thoughts for a while. My father had fallen down at death. I don't know if he broke anything.

Since it was apparent he didn't think of me in life, my dream asked: did he think of me in death?

1977

"One Miss-is-sippi, two Miss-is-sippi, three Miss-is-sippi, four Miss-is-

sippi, five!

Ready or not, here I come…"

I was always a little timid when it was my turn to seek. I was four years old, and the thought of being alone petrified me. What if I didn't find them? What if they're in a really good hiding spot? What if they jumped out and scared me first?

"Gotcha!" I yelled. There were only three of us. I found my little cousin behind the door first. My sister, Mo, was too old to play with me, Chris, and Lil Dawud. Roberta let us have the other bedroom and the living room; no one was allowed to play in the kitchen or her room.

"Found you!"

"Now it's your turn to hide!"

We scattered about and tried to be creative hiding in only two rooms. We always hushed each other to be quiet and "get in your own spot." You didn't want to be the last one when, "…ready or not, here I come…"

Roberta's living room was poorly lit. It had large dark green velvet furniture, rose print wallpaper, a blood-red Oriental rug with floor to ceiling burgundy and white curtains. I wished I could pull the drapes back to bring in the sunshine, but I knew she would ring me around like a rag doll if I did. I crawled behind the sofa and remained super still. My older cousin, Chris, was seeking this time. He liked to tickle me with every find, so I really didn't want him to find me. I stayed motionless. After about two or three minutes, both boys were still looking for me, and they alerted Roberta.

She yelled, "Sunny! You better get your little behind out here where I can see you…"

I couldn't stand up, so I had to scurry back to the corner, and by that time, she spotted me. Roberta pointed and said, "No more playing behind the sofa!"

"Then we don't have any good places to hi—"

"Did you hear me, Sunny?"

"Yea—but it's not any fun…"

"What did I say?"

"Yes, Roberta. No playing behind the sofa."

After that, we just stood and looked at each other and silently questioned, what now?

Every other weekend, we would meet our cousins at our grandmother's house. She usually baked bread from scratch. I would watch, Mo got to help. Roberta would listen to AM radio in the kitchen, mostly 1010 WINS. She wasn't the most affectionate. I don't have any memories of her hugs or kisses. She wasn't the one who baked cookies and took you to the store to buy what you wanted. She was more of the make-sure-you-don't-hurt-yourself-while-running type of grandma. "Put your hand back in the car" type grandma and the "call me Roberta" type grandma. She worked a nine-to-five while my mother's mother did not, so we perceived her as well-off. I don't know how she got the every other weekend duty of watching the grandkids, but it was noticeable she didn't really like it.

Our other cousin, Garnet, was older and lived downstairs with my great-grandmother and great-grandfather. They adopted her since Garnet's mother was mentally ill. It was the family's greatest remorse; I heard her mother lived under a bridge. Garnet was my favorite. With gentle care and imagination, she would sometimes let me play with the paper dolls in her room. We would dress them up to meet with friends and go shopping at the mall and then get them undressed to go to bed. Paper dolls were better than any cartoon television show. Garnet never came upstairs, so the boys and I got to play upstairs with Roberta. While Mo stayed downstairs with Garnet.

If it were really hot, we got to go outside and get hosed off on the cement driveway, and the younger ones got to splash in the kiddie pool. They all said, once I was old enough to play, the pool got "too crowded."

Inside, we either played House, Duck, Duck, Goose, Ring Around the Rosie, Simon Says (my favorite), Red-Light, Green-Light, or Hide and Seek. We couldn't play Tag in the house and, sometimes, if Ring Around the Rosie got too loud, that game would get shut down too. One thing we knew for sure: no running games.

Mo was six years older, my little mother. So, if I was four, she was ten. Way too old to "play with the babies," she would say. Christopher was seven, almost eight, and Lil Dawud was three. I was just excited I got to tag along. The boys liked to jump, kick, and give each other bear hugs that became rolling on the floor with somebody hurt. Most of the time it was Lil Dawud, but he wouldn't say anything. The boys liked to playhouse with me as the baby. Chris always played Daddy and Dawud was usually the neighbor or the friend who knocked on the door. Part of the fun was telling the neighbor to "hold on a minute."

Since I was young, I was the baby bouncing on Daddy's lap and always facing him so I could fake cry on his chest. One time, I felt a bulge in his pocket and paused and looked. He pulled me, roughly, back up on his lap and rocked his legs around, all the while telling me to shush. I felt it again, but this time he didn't let me move. By the time Dawud "came to the door," Chris wanted to carry me around his waist. I never minded it before, but something about this time irked me. Still, I kept playing.

Next time we played House, we changed up characters, and I was the mommy for the first time. Chris was Daddy, as always, and Lil Dawud was the next-door neighbor who needed a cup of sugar. He waited outside the room for a few minutes before knocking.

Chris said, "Mommy always gets naked in front of Daddy..." He pulled down my tube top without asking, exposing my baby chest and nipples. I remember just standing there, looking down. "Now let me see your..." He motioned with his lips and chin.

I wiggled out of my shorts and kept them around my ankles as he hugged me. When Dawud knocked, Chris yelled, "Just a minute, be right there," which gave me enough time to pull up my shorts, adjust my top, and feel shame for the first time.

Before bed that night, I recall Mo asking to change the sleeping arrangements. I don't know why she didn't want to sleep with me. She said I

76

snored and wiggled around too much. I ended up on the pull-out couch next to Chris.

He whispered, "Daddy's here, baby. Or will you play Mommy tonight?"

I cringed and hoped I didn't have to feel the bulge in his pocket. A few minutes after Roberta turned off the living room and bedroom lights, she got in her bed with four creaks and a moan.

Chris quickly rolled on top of me. He covered my mouth, held his finger over his lips and told me, "Shhhh!" He was heavy and was hurting me. His pajama pants were loose, so I could feel the shape of the bulge. It was like a banana; I'll never forget. It was poking me through my Wonder Woman/Justice League underwear and flimsy nightgown.

Roberta heard me struggle. "What are you two doing up?" He released his hold and I yelled, "Roberta, I need to..."

She didn't get up, she just turned on her side table light as he slowly slid off to my left. I could see her sitting up in bed.

"Roberta, I need a..." I didn't know what to say.

"What is it now?"

"Can I get a glass of wat—"

"No." She got angry at me for talking after "lights out" and wouldn't let me finish.

"Good night, Sunny!"

"But Roberta, I—"

"I said good night. We'll talk in the morning."

I didn't say anything in the morning. The next night, I wanted to sleep with Roberta by any means necessary. I didn't allow her to say no. I was already in her room and under the covers. I remember the look Chris gave me; I could see him on the pull-out couch next to Lil Dawud as she went to turn off the light. He never touched me again after that night. I don't know if it was my reaction—or if it was just that close to my parent's divorce that

77

we didn't go over there anymore.

September 17th, 2019

Benjamin had one elusive friend, Derrick. He was a gamer and appreciated spending time with Benjamin alone, gaming. He mocked our relationship and asked, "Why would a woman of her age have anything to do with YOU!?"

Benjamin, also a gamer, enjoyed several hours zoned out, transported to another world where the controller allowed him to succeed and win at life or try again. Defeat is part of the game, and the only challenge is to trump one's high score. Their fierce competitive nature matched intensely, and Benjamin never questioned why Derrick preferred their time together to be alone.

Not until his name had been mentioned in conversation a few times did I inquire about meeting Derrick. The night before the set meeting Tabitha warned me, "He's an asshole." So, I approached him with prejudice. Much to my dismay, when we met, he was pleasant and entertaining. He asked questions to understand the depth of our relationship and he was taken aback when I told him, "I've known Benji for years."

"Really?"

Actually, I knew Benjamin longer. I was in the lead; he had to concede our relationship could actually be based on something. Our humor was both quick and dry borderline sarcastic. Derrick admitted he intentionally waited to meet me to see if it would last. I was getting the same response from my mother, so I understood.

After a pretty chill night with Derrick, I reported back to Tabitha: "He was charming and funny." She swore I met "his representative" and said, "Wait! You'll see."

September 18th, 2020

Brooklyn-born Ruth Bader Ginsberg will forever be remembered as the first Jewish female Supreme Court Justice. She died at eighty-seven, teaching little girls and women, anything you put your mind towards you can achieve. She was known for many quotes but one that stands out was,

"Fight for the things you care about. But do it in a way others will join you."
RBG (13)

September 19th, 2020

After my father's funeral service, I decided not to go back to Roberta's house for the repass. She invited me over the next weekend to "talk about things." She lived at 1313 Redrum Drive, New Brunswick, New Jersey. It was my first time walking into the house since 2000. It was not the house of my childhood memories. Her and my father lived there alone, since she told Sharon, my aunt, and her only daughter, to leave. My cousin Christopher lived in the attic but was kicked out for weapons possession and terrorist threats. Dawud never lived there; he went into the Army and made a career out of it. He lived in Kuwait for about a decade until recently moving to North Carolina to get married. We remained friends and talked more than any other of my father's family. Christopher never married, no children and no one knows his current whereabouts. Roberta's been in this house since 1990 and now lives alone.

Signs of weather, overdue repairs, and neglect were evident. She invited me to sit down with her on the low and dirty couch. I complimented her on being quick on her feet for a ninety-three-year-old.

"I'm ninety-four."

"Oh, excuse me..."

"It's okay. I walk, stretch, and do yoga every day. Well, not every day but four to five times a week."

"That's excellent! My other grandmother can't walk and uses a wheelchair. So, I definitely take my hat off to you for finding the fountain of youth."

She smiled. "How are your grandmother and your mother? She must've been devastated." She wrongfully assumed her beloved son would be missed by his first abused wife.

I kept the truth to myself. "Actually, my grandmother is doing okay today. Thank you for asking. She just doesn't have her strength...and my mother? She's really good. Yeap, she's doing well for herself." As I nodded my head.

"Oh! Because I always worried about you... and your mother and sister. How are Mo's girls? Girls, right?"

My sister is turning in her...urn right now. She despised this woman and "your father," as she would call him. Roberta knows nothing about Mo's children because Mo cut all ties in the early 80s.

I forced a pause before I answered, "Mo has two grown and beautiful daughters." I rushed the last part because I knew she really didn't care. "They live in Florida...but what were the things you wanted to talk about?"

"Well, as you may know, Mark and Sharon were on the deed of the house with me. And since I haven't seen or heard from Sharon in seven or eight years, I was thinking...Do you want the house?"

I didn't want to seem ungrateful, so I answered without much thought, "Sure. I would love to inherit the house."

"I mean, I would have to get a lawyer to put your name along with mine on the deed."

I don't know my grandmother. For a woman I've only seen once in forty years, she was being awfully generous. Guilt has a funny way of displaying itself.

Once I drove away, I imagined a show like Love it or List it coming in and restoring the old house. Except Roberta would have to be on Hoarders first before any remake or demolition show. Of course, I wanted a fully paid-off house with good bones in an up-and-coming suburban neighborhood. I thought about all the dumpsters and guys I would have to hire to clean the house and help me move in. I dreamt about gutting out the first floor to open up more space on the second.

September 23rd

No Justice for Breonna Taylor.

Or were the cops just doing their job?

No Justice? No Peace.

It's a fascinating time in America today. The pandemic's death toll exceeds 200,000. There is a financial crisis due to closed businesses, and massive amounts of Americans are out of work. Injustice and inequity plagued by the darker-skinned Americans who've fought since slavery, Jim Crow, and the Reagan-era. Non-stop protests have erupted all over the country in Portland, Minneapolis, Chicago, and New York, to name a few.

With protest comes looting quickly starts riots which means more police, tear gas, and military presence. We are at a place of civil unrest—

I heard, "The same people who don't want us to protest systemic racism in America are the same ones who started a war to keep us enslaved." ~unknown.

With this election looming—I hope we all make it home alive.

September 30th

Senator Democratic Leader Chuck Schumer (D-NY) today spoke on the Senate floor decrying President Trump's refusal to condemn white supremacist groups.

"Last night, President Trump delivered one of the most disgraceful performances at a presidential debate that anyone has ever seen. And I don't mean that from a political perspective, I mean it from a human perspective.

One can endure the President's tendencies to meltdown when confronted with his facts. His brazen lack of self-awareness, his stunning lack of regard for others but it was maddening to watch the President last night, angry and small, unable to show a scintilla of respect, unable to follow even the basic rules of human civility or decorum. Unwilling to constrain a stream of obvious falsehoods and right wing vile.

Shakespeare summed up in Macbeth, Trump's performance last night, a tale told by an idiot full of Sound and Fury signifying nothing.

Yes, President Trump's debate performance was in the words of Macbeth, a tale told by an idiot of sound and fury signifying nothing.

In an hour and a half that felt like a lifetime, the president managed to insult Vice President Biden's deceased son and smear a living one, please a fringe white supremacist group, and capped the night off by yet again casting doubt on our own elections—tarnishing our own democracy.

Those were just his worst moments. The rest of the debate saw the president heap lie upon lie; lies big and small and every size in between.

The president and truth don't intersect at all.

Still, one moment stands out. Asked to condemn white supremacist groups like the "Proud Boys" —classified a hate group by the Southern Poverty Law Center, called "hard core white supremacists" by the anti-Defamation League—President Trump demurred and then said: "Proud Boys —stand back and stand by."

Stand back and stand by?

President Obama once wondered, rhetorically, 'How hard is it to say the Nazis are bad?' Apparently, for President Trump, it is beyond his capacity..." (14)

CHAPTER SIX

We are living through history. Masks are government mandated now; restaurants open to 25% capacity then close back down again. Schools go remote, proms, and graduations are destroyed. For kids across the world school just stopped. Left millions of parents to create a home school and question: how do we go back to work with no childcare? Zoom meetings replace in-person, and life as we know it is obliterated. The judgment and the stare you give someone if they were seen outside with pajamas on is long gone. The pajama pants are the new black; they go with everything. The pajama suit is trending and so is the elbow "handshake," the air hug, the 6-foot glare you give someone standing too close.

The oddest report: The sky over Manhattan is clear. A movie scene would best describe riding down the FDR Drive then cutting across midtown in seventeen minutes. No jackhammers, no ambulances, or motorcycles, no crosstown, midtown, or downtown buses, no one yelling "TAX-EE," no food trucks, hotdog or newspaper stands, no delis open 24 hours, no underground rumble of the E, F and G trains, no connecting to the four, five, and six lines. No Broadway. No whistles of the doormen. No swoosh of the bikes, no roar of the 1,568 passing cars, no police lights. No meter maids or crossing guards, no traffic at all. Peace and quiet—apocalyptic, even.

Donald Trump's story continues in the White House with the election of the decade. Millions vote; the country is completely divided down a sliver of a line. Kamala Harris, soon-to-be the first everything, is in the White House making little Black girls and women proud.

Hurricane storms have not stopped. With named storms finished, scientists move to the Greek alphabet. One of the storms even comes back a second time—something never before seen or heard of in history. California still burns and the soon-NOT-to-be President still refuses to concede. With no vaccine as of yet, the second wave hits with fresh curfews, stay-at-home orders for Thanksgiving, and the Times Square New Year's Eve celebration? Canceled.

My heart breaks for all the people trying to cope with this devastation and the mental toll.

November 26th, 2020

Chicago rapper, King Von dies from gun violence at the height of his career. He was only 26. (15)

Trump has yet to concede. When questioned in an interview he answered, "Certainly, I will (leave)—and you know that," Donald Trump said in an interview. "But I think that there will be a lot of things happening between now and the 20th of January, a lot of things."(16)

We'll see.

Cardi B dons the cover of Billboard with Billboard's 2020 Woman of the Year just after breaking records for being the first person to twice win the American Music Award for Best Rap Song of the Year. She's quoted, "I like Justice. But I also like popping my pussy."

April 2019

I used the Facebook platform to share and ask for aid in my torture and fear. I posted my GoFundMe page detailing King Shaburger's whereabouts and my next steps of tactical training. The page first showed the post he made a collage of me: half-naked, two pictures of me eating with a pig ears and snout filter, and then me relaxing on the couch after an exhausting day. Actually, nothing was wrong with that picture—it just wasn't my best light. He titled it, "My Baby Piggie, the fat get fatter." He sent it to a few co-workers, random friends, and my mom. Under the photos I told the story of our fast and super quick romance. From falling for the "wrong guy," avoiding the red flags, to the night he came to my house, drunk, with intent to harm me. How he put me in the hospital and continued to throw bricks at my front windows. Though I assured them he was incarcerated, he would also soon be out—and I believed him as he reassured me, he would be back. I implored anyone who would listen for financial help with the needed purchases to safeguard my family.

Most just looked, some commented with disbelief and "thoughts and prayers." A surprising number of women disagreed with my decision and offered to help if I moved instead. A handful donated. Only one went out of their way with a 400-dollar contribution, saying she had been in a similar situation and could sympathize with my pain. She requested to remain anonymous. (Class of '91/LAG for LIFE!)

One other person stepped forward and offered his time and knowledge. We never met, but he heard my story from a mutual friend; she was appalled at the turmoil I was going through. He asked if I was committed to learning how to protect my family, by any means necessary. When I answered, "Yes!" he drove to Jersey from Queens and brought his arsenal of long guns and handguns. We met at the range he swore by in Woodland Park. Just after 45 minutes of instruction, my first two shots were dead center, only a crosshair from each other.

Before going home, I went to Family Dollar to show Benjamin my target practice. He was so excited, he called to his closest co-worker, "My baby went to the range!" She smiled and nodded. The older black man standing in line was impressed and gave a thumbs-up.

November 17th 2019

Number 1.5 on the list was to meet the family. Benjamin and I have known each other for over ten years, and on his birthday, I met his entire family for the first time. There was the sister, who lived upstate and only came down on holidays and birthdays. The mother, who told Benjamin she could hear me. His father, who I'd met before, usually caught smiling and sitting in the kitchen at night. Then there was his brother, who I'd only met in passing. He was the one constantly yelling, "Benji, there's someone parked in my spot!" He and I had never met face-to-face. This was the first time I looked at him directly; he was hard on the eyes. Six-ten, close to 500 pounds, out-grown beard, and bushy hair around his ears since the top ceased growing years ago. He was lighter than the rest of the family. He looked mostly like his father, light skin, coke bottle glasses and bald. Even though the whole family wore glasses. The sister, as Ben told me, was the real person to impress, since she was more caring and attentive than his actual mother. She was fifteen years older, so she was his "lil' mom".

85

Admiring her long hair fixed in a loose bun, I asked, "How long have you been growing your dreadlocks?"

She looked at me, paused for a moment, and said, "I don't have dreadlocks. These are locs and I've been growing them for seven years."

"Excuse me, I wasn't aware there was a difference."

"No worries. Most people who haven't traveled this journey don't. When the Africans were brought in ships, laying down for months and not having showers or room to move; their hair would mat. So, when they finally got off the boat the Americans, seeing this for the first time, would say, 'Oh My Lord, they're hair is dreadful.' There's nothing dreadful about my hair."

(Locs are neatly manicured and maintained usually done by a professional loctician.)

I nodded in place of words with much respect due.

Benjamin warned me earlier—he was his parents' only hope for grandchildren since his brother, forty-two, and his sister, fifty-four, decided they weren't having any heirs. He said they might ask me about wanting more children, especially since his last relationship was with a lesbian. They were best friends who married to prevent her from having to leave the country. The fake ceremony had to appear real in pictures, so his family threw them a party with all his friends and her immediate family.

Technically, they were still married but, of course, strictly on paper. He had told me about her before, but every time it was brought up in conversation, it took me by surprise. Just sounded weird: his wife.

Thankfully, I made it through lunch without being asked any embarrassing questions, and they appeared cordial, whatever that meant. His dad liked me already. He appreciated my appearance, Ben said, because I was light skin with large breasts. It seemed as if Dad was easily satisfied. Mom was just happy to put a face to the obtrusive moaning noises. His sister seemed to enjoy my conversation and kept the banter going. His brother now took it as a personal challenge to see who would park in "his spot" first and sometimes greeted me by yelling, "Thanks for not parking in my spot."

His family was scratched off the list. Now, my mother is a difficult human who lives by her own accord. She flat-out refused to meet Benjamin. She said it was too soon after the last fiasco of a relationship I had. Her PTSD from that didn't allow her any space to meet anyone new. Especially when she heard Benjamin was a 36-year-old man who lived in his parent's basement, worked at Family Dollar, and didn't drive. I tried to explain we were in love; she wouldn't hear it. Benjamin understood, or he appeared to, and we moved on.

Ben's birthday party that night was in the basement which smelled of mold—most likely, drainage problems. He lit candles and sprayed Febreze shortly before anyone arrived. His bedroom consisted of two futons, L-shaped, with two 40-inch televisions across from them. The bed we slept on faced the staircase. So, as you came down, there was the bathroom and storage to your right and a couple of fold-up chairs and the laundry room to the left. It was basically a studio apartment.

The basement's maximum capacity was definitely exceeded with the ebb and flow of faces. Karim and Tab, of course, were in attendance, Keith, Daysun, and even Daisy made an appearance. Adrian from Family Dollar, Derrick and a few other dudes stopped by.

I was so drunk and blurred out that I can't remember. I do recall posing for a picture, facing Benjamin on my knees as he held two large bottles of E&J. But now as I look back, I am intrigued how I allowed myself there, in a room surrounded by men, sitting on the exact bed we sexed on, with two other girls to witness.

By the end of the night, I got belligerent and rowdy. I definitely exceeded my limit. I thought my rudeness was funny and my abrupt speech was even warranted. At one point, Karim made a toast, "To Ben, always Momma's boy—but never quite a man."

Ben laughed and threw back his cup. I took offense and said, "You're in his house, pay him some respect!" Everyone looked up in alarm.

Karim was already standing, he took a step forward, "Are you serious?"

"Yes! You just offended him."

Ben tried to interject, "No, you didn't" as he turned to me, "He was just joking…"

"No! He was being an asshole and insulted you to your face in your own home!"

"What did I even say?" Karim asked me.

"Yea! What did he say?!" Derrick chimes in.

Now I'm off course, "I don't know… something about his mother…"

"No, the fuck, I did not!" As he raised his voice to combat me.

"No! He didn't!" Derrick was the sounding board.

"He was joking," Benjamin reassured me.

"You said, he was a little boy living in his mother's house" I yelled and trying to make what he honestly said sound worse for the argument. "Now—apologize." I stood up behind Ben.

"What?" Karim looked at me with pure confusion.

"No. You don't have to apologize…" Benjamin put his hands out in an attempt to calm the situation.

"You heard what I said, apologize to him." As I was sure my point was valid.

"I think something's wrong with you…you don't want to start a fight with me." Karim said with a smirk.

Derrick blurted out, "Yea! You're fucked up."

There were a few sounds of disbelief and dismay, but the room was quiet except now the music was too loud. The onlookers watched like a tennis match, and I could feel a tingle of a headache coming on.

"I wasn't talking to you…" pointing at Derrick then pivoted and said, "You must think I'm scared." They both stood in silence with a jaw adjustment, looked at each other and then back at me.

Karim moved quickly. I didn't flinch but thank goodness Derrick was standing by because he reacted swiftly enough to step Karim back.

The party was over. It was unfortunate Ben felt he needed to apologize for me. I heard him say something like, "Excuse her, she just had too much to drink…" But by that time, I was excited and amped for some more action. Everyone took turns picking up their coats to leave. I looked at them like, what happened? Karim looked back as a few pushed him away. I could hear him say, "You lucky this time." I was instructed to stay inside to allow him time to leave. I felt no pain and was not bothered. I laughed at the outcome and encouraged anyone else to "come for me."

That party will go down in infamy with me being the raging alcoholic and another "one" that doesn't know to hold their liquor. I heard later they saw signs of narcissism and thought I was delusional; my alcohol and cocaine abuse was aggressive.

A couple days later, I drove to Ben's house hoping he had forgiven me. Since it was raining, he and I smoked in the Jeep. He wasn't talking much, and that new song just dropped by Pop Smoke; the beat and hook are crazy. I turned it up to sing along.

"Christian Dior, Dior/ I'm up in all the stores/ when it rain it pours/ she like the way that I dance/ she like the way that I move/ she like the way that I rock/ she like the way that I woo/ she let it clap for a nig—"

He shushed me as he turned down the radio. I gave him a double-what with a side eye.

"It can't be too loud; my mom is home."

December 2nd

Karim and everyone agreed to forgive me and cut me some slack. It was obvious I was intoxicated so we let a few nights go by without hanging out to let everything cool off. But on this one night, Ben and I were alone in the middle of an episode of Ozark. We both wanted more "Britney Spears," so he texted Karim. He responded quickly and said he'd be there shortly. I told Ben to "let me handle this," as we were both convinced, he gave me *more. When Karim got there, he instinctively sat at the "round table."*

He texted Ben, "outside."

I went upstairs to meet him and exchange money for drugs.

It was after 9pm and it was dark as I walked up on him, he was startled but smiled. He stood up and turned to face me. I walked past him to make him turn again. I talked softly about him not being trusted and needed to know if he had weapons or sharp objects. I pulled his arms up and started to frisk him. Spread his legs with my one foot and patted him down. He grinned with all his teeth as I told him to "Hold still or I might get poked. Any sharp objects?" He was fully engaged and delighted at the opportunity to kiss me. Out from behind the shadows Benjamin appears, I had to push Karim away from my face. His lips were milliseconds off of mine. Karim looked up and asked, "Am I being ambushed?" I scoffed, as Ben walked past us in total respect for the deal. He talked fast and we exchanged what I think was a gram for sixty dollars. I happily paid as he mumbled some words too far away to hear. He kept walking as we both smiled back at each other.

Back inside we began to organize the drugs when my phone rang. I reached in my pocket and paused at the name. "It's HIM!" I yelled. Shaburger had been calling me all day. I refused to answer. I could feel blood throbbing through the veins in my wrist as I held the phone. Benjamin looked at me inquisitively as it rang again.

"That stupid motherfucker who should be in jail right now!"

Benjamin looked comfortable and said, "Let me handle this..." as he reached out his hand.

RING! "He's going to lie; he's going to say bad things...he's going to—"

He touched my hand, and I relaxed my grip. "Hello?"

"Who's this?!" I could hear the irritation in his voice through the phone.

"Benjamin—"

"Who the fuck are you? What kind of black man is named Benjamin?

You don't have the knowledge of self to be called a King. You're not a black man, you're a...You know what? Fuck this—" Then he hung up.

We sat in silence for a few moments. As we, both, were shaken.

"Thank you." I leaned in to kiss him on the cheek. He nodded as his sweat glands had already activated to cool him down. It took a few more deep breaths to regain his resting heart rate.

I blocked and deleted Shaburger's number again.

CHAPTER SEVEN

December 7th, 2020

The second surge is amongst us as "they" promised. A vaccine is "on its way" from Pfizer. Thanksgiving has turned into Christmas with most Americans shopping and decorating right after Halloween. The economic upswing has people spending their money on Christmas commercialism and digging deep into debt for the must-haves of the season. Travel bans and family bans with restrictions on the number of people you choose to have in your own home has everyone everywhere in Pandemic Fatigue, not knowing if it's the worst of times or the best of times, just wishing it was over. The collective consensus is we all would rather be talking about the year 2020 through distant memories than living in it. It can be seen as the time when families got closer, relationships were challenged, and the strong emerged. The weak, feeble, old, and poor-conditioned stayed home; it was easier to lessen the chance of illness.

The construction on my new place was finished; the earliest I could move in was December 7th. I wasn't able to see it until that day. My ensuite was to die for and the walk-in closet is of my dreams. I really couldn't complain. I was blessed. I was number six on the list of inquiries and guaranteed a spot, as long as I had all of the paperwork concerning my last three years of taxes, good credit, business forms, and bank receipts. My side hustle was taken into consideration since I was bringing in a couple hundred dollars a month. Thankfully, it allowed me in the building. Unfortunately, COVID put a stop to that money. I was grateful I put all this in motion before I met Shaburger. I will not complain because life could be none and for those who are not here, I count my blessings. I felt safe and therefore grateful. The lease renewal went along with a breeze.

The first time Benjamin saw the place, he acted unaffected.

I asked, "So how do you like it?" He answered, "It's okay."

"It's, okay?!" I blurted.

"Yeah... it's not like you bought a spider monkey or anything...then

I would've been impressed. It's an apartment. It's okay."

I nodded with assurance, "Oh-kay."

From then on, I stopped asking if my blessings were good enough for other people.

December 20th 2019

As I reflect, this is the same time King Shaburger was released from Bourbon County after serving six weeks of his three-month sentence. He was home in time for Christmas. He called sporadically. I never accepted the collect calls but by the end of year, I opted to change my 646 number to the 551-area code. Shortly after, I received a text from a random number.

It read "Happy Holidays."

Since I didn't know, I asked, "Who's this?"

I received a picture from somewhere in sunny Brooklyn looking like nothing bothers Shaburger. He said he only wanted to apologize, there was no need for the police. He pleaded with me for closure, because his mother, who art in heaven, needed him to do this which made me shake my head in disbelief.

I read his six paragraph-length texts twice and headed to the Westfield Precinct. Upon arrival, they questioned my whereabouts, when I received said messages, and why I didn't contact the local police.

"I was on my way home. I stopped to read them—but aren't you closer to my house? And wouldn't you need to know this man is still harassing me?"

One sucked his teeth and the other rolled his eyes. The officer in front breathed heavily and said, "I guess I'll start the paperwork..."

I was confused—wasn't that their job?

They wanted screenshots emailed to the sergeant in charge. Then, they thanked me without much reassurance of what would happen next. I had a feeling, if anyone was going to be aware of my surroundings, it would have to be me. I called again the number given for the gun license to push for my application status. I continued my research on handguns for security and knew I had about 500 saved for the Sig Sauer 1-9-11 Emperor Scorpion Full-Size. It is light yet powerful. I felt assured I could handle myself in any situation.

Days later, Shaburger sent a message to my mother on Facebook, something like, "Tell your fat, disgusting daughter to have a Merry Christmas! To the both of you fucking nasty hoes!" I deleted my Facebook account and moved into my apartment right before he knew where to look. My mother amped up her cameras, bought a 6-foot gate with a lock, and another motion sensor light for the alleyway. I felt safe, especially with my new switchblades, bear spray, and personal alarm for my keychain. He wants me? Let him come get me. I promise I'm not the same person he left.

April 15th, 2020

A few months after settling in, my peace was again disturbed by new upstairs neighbors. Their children were obviously small because they ran quickly. I'd say boys, only because once the heavy furniture was moved in, the running and jumping started. I predicted they were a little older than toddlers because they settled down right around 8:30 every night. They would run, jump, slide, and crash right after school—no wonder they would fall into bed. It was disturbing but bearable. I shook my head often knowing from experience little boys were full of energy and extremely boisterous.

PSE&G sent us home four months into the year with loaned company computers and headsets. They said we were essential workers, which was hard to fathom. We felt the true gravity of COVID when the National Basketball Association stopped all games. I went home to share my palatial abode with my high school-aged sons. My oldest, Cue, graduated Class of 2020 with no prom, no walk across the stage, and no fanfare except for a wall-sized poster of his graduation photo on the school's fence. Thai continued his sophomore and junior year from the comfort of his bed. My email rang out for requests to see his face, see his work, and see his advancements. I was tired for him and could only imagine being home and still hating school.

It was a time for me to reflect on myself and be at one with the core things. No more running around trying to fill my day with activities, work, people, or shopping. Everyday tasks were done from home. Amazon shopping ramped up. Uber Eats and Grubhub made me aware I was going to gain weight here if I didn't find a way to keep moving. "COVID-20" referred to the twenty pounds people packed on from being sedentary. I started belly dancing with the women on YouTube. The music just made me want to dance and, if I could look like that, move like that, I would come out of this better not worse.

Cue went into the United States Marines Corps a couple months after graduation. That left Thai and me to binge-watch Netflix. I twisted my hair out of sheer boredom and not wanting to wake up and look at bedhead all day/every day. We started watching seasons upon seasons of shows, intertwined with five different comedy stand-ups. Hands down— Chappelle's series kept me going, as well as Marlon Wayans' WOKEish (Class of '90). He is living his life to its fullest. His "Thank You"'s were touching as I knew a few of the people he honored as he also did shout out LAG.

We started watching everything from Explained to psychedelic documentaries, with the occasional Hulu visit for Rick and Morty. Bird Box was a big hit; it fell in line with what we were going through. Don't Look Up was an extreme satire on our situation. My 16-year-old and I enjoyed evenings on the terrace vibing to Lil Dirk, Gunna, NLE Choppa, Ski Mask the Slump God, Juice WRLD, and the Migos. We smoked together, we talked, we laughed, we bonded. He grew up in front of my eyes and I was astounded.

Unfortunately, at the beginning of the lockdown, Thai left a few times after I closed my door to go to sleep. God woke me up one night as he called to his brother, "Let me in. Ma locked the top lock." I walked into the living room at the same moment Cue stepped toward the entryway. I questioned him and he told me Thai was outside. I opened the door first. Thai was terrified and anticipated me hitting him. He stood in the hallway a second too long and I manhandled him, grabbed his arm, ushered him in, and led him to the couch. I remember my heart racing and the deep breath I took before I gave him two options: "The morning flight or evening? Because your dad needs to know what time to pick you up from the airport." After the threat of going to live with his father in South Carolina, his whole demeanor changed.

Instead of sneaking around with his friends, I offered our apartment as a safe space for him. We became smoke buddies to maintain the peace in my house.

One night, I was startled by the sound of something major falling to the floor. I heard a loud thud in the corner of the living room. My attention shifted, and I stared at the ceiling as if I could see through it. A man's voice could be heard in baritone. I watched the ceiling because that's all I knew. I was perplexed. I hadn't heard him until now. He was very demanding; I couldn't make out his words, but they were argumentative. I waited for a response, but the ceiling held no clues. When a noise much louder bounced off the inner wall, I was frightened for the people upstairs. What should I do? Who should I call? I listened and heard voices moving into the bedroom. I was worried. Should I follow them? I turned off all electrical devices and anything with a hum, highly anticipating more. Moments later, I heard the man again. I followed the sound of his footsteps with my gaze. His shoes pressed loud into the carpet. His feet were quick and heavy. I imagined him breaking into a slight run to catch up to someone fleeing. My heart felt quick and heavy with his steps. I prayed for peace as there was a moment of silence. There was another rush into the bathroom. I finally heard a woman's voice muffled with tears. He was at the door telling her he was sorry. "Come out so I could..." he trailed off and lowered his voice. I waited for more and sat in silence for a while. Not every night, maybe once a week, I could hear and feel his presence.

Monday evening, around eleven o'clock, I went to lie down. The sound this time was different. He broadcasted his intention to kill her right above my bed. I jumped to a seated position and listened as if it were an opera. I didn't understand their words, but I could comprehend from the rise and fall of their voice levels and pitch. I wondered what would happen next. In sheer disbelief, I hung on to every muffled turn, pound on the door, and weight drop. I questioned why the woman upstairs hadn't called out in pain or yelled for help, but I also understood her children would be the first to run and try to help. So, I called the police because my PTSD wouldn't allow me to listen any longer.

I let two days pass and went upstairs to confront the woman with the boisterous children. Their running and jumping reached a fever pitch.

96

I went with my African cloth as a face mask for decency. She answered the knock with a delay.

"Who is it?" As she looked through the peephole.

"Your downstairs neighbor..." The crack in the door was just enough to expose her brown skin and long thin locs. She stood at 5'10" and was in need of a sandwich. "Hi! I'm Sunny, your downstairs neighbor...I came up to let you know I hear you."

She took a brief pause to collect her thoughts and nodded.

"I was wondering if everyone's ok...because it's really loud and sounds like running and jumping."

"Oh yes—" she smiled, exposing her teeth, "I have small children..."

"Yes, I'm aware. I was wondering if you could let them know they have a downstairs neighbor that works from home..."

"Sure, I will let them know. My apologies. Was there anything else?" Said with a hover-face as she waited for me to walk away.

"I was just checking to see if everyone is ok because it does get loud, and I am concerned."

"Yes. Everyone is fine, thank you..." She gave me an annoyed smirk.

"You're welcome. Nice meeting you."

I decided to walk away without giving her the hotline number for domestic violence I brought with me.

October 6th

I was weak and searched for companionship online. It felt like the connections never went further than a sexually explicit dialogue. My body was itching, longing for strangers to fill a void. I poked the African, my IG crush. He was easy and invited me over for our second meeting. He again requested that I "come naked." This time I obliged. Under the trench was a micro mini exposing my red panties, bra, and a sheer top for decorum. He wasn't that excited when I had booty cheeks out; bent down to take my shoes off. He wanted to sit, watch television, and talk. We sat and talked about things and life. When I mentioned I was penning a book, he asked if it was my second. When I answered, "No, my first," he blew me off with a sound of disinterest and boredom. The sex wasn't as good, his kink fetishes were off, and he seemed more like a want-to-be boyfriend than a good, stiff fuckbuddy. I was turned off and immediately remembered why it had been a few months.

I could feel myself coming undone from the stress of COVID. Staying indoors and thinking of things as a potential threat can make you sick and potentially kill you. There's a fear of loss, fear of losing family, friends, work, your home. I thought of self-medicating with Valium. Wouldn't that make things so much easier?

Home became a haven for most, until the news of domestic cases where children were reported going hungry during the quarantine. School breakfast and lunches were a loss for some parents. My town started a pop-up drive-thru food pantry supplying groceries to those in need with school-aged children.

Our local newspaper, The Suburbanite, ran a story on the Bourbon County schools and the percentage of children possibly doing without.

December 20th

Dr. Kizzmekia Corbett, a Black woman, is a viral immunologist at the forefront of developing the Moderna vaccine. (17)

December 25th

Happy Heavenly Birthday, Monique. I still hold the Christmas/Birthday card I forgot to mail to you. It's funny and it makes me laugh. I don't remember the joke off hand, but the punchline is "Pick One." Get it? Because there's only one card. You would've liked it and called me by now.

Later that week

Shondra Rhimes' Bridgerton on Netflix inspired my British accent to come out for six straight weeks. I couldn't wait for the follow-up.

HAPPY NEW YEAR!

2020 is in the past. There's a renewed sense of gratitude amongst the living and worldwide sigh of relief.

January 6th, 2021

This day will go down in infamy. Extremists and the Proud Boys stormed the Capitol under what looked like the direction and guidance of the sitting president, Donald Trump.

I imagine "This is America" by Childish Gambino playing in the background.

CHAPTER EIGHT

2020 is over, yet still reverberating. Going outside without good reason is still ill advised.

Within the painted, light gray walls adorned with pictures and artifacts, sometimes the eye catches a painting or a mirror or the time. I can do nothing but clean every surface area twice daily. Disinfectant wipes and hand sanitizer on deck. I am heavily grateful and understand this is a gift that I do not take lightly. My home is beautiful, my children are taken care of, and I am blessed. I meditate and thank the universe. I imagine I have the capability of manifesting the life I want. I only need to trust and believe.

1983

My Gaga, my mom's grandma, adored me with hugs, side-cheek kisses, and good food.

Her love was different. Her apartment was well lit with no doors closed to play. She loved to read magazines and imagine faraway places. We sat and talked for hours, sipping on our hot Nescafe' and munching on Nilla Wafers in the delicate cup and saucer set.

She would sometimes take me to work with her on my days off from school.

She helped clean a condominium on the 38th floor of the Tracey Towers. I loved going with her. She would keep little candies in her pockets for the ride and tell stories of her childhood recalling her grandparents as slaves and how her Uncle Barry fought in the Civil War. She was reminiscent of 1865, a time I could never fully visualize. Cape Charles, Virginia was her home, and the family still had a plot of land in the Bay area. I asked numerous questions and she never tired of me. I was so curious how she moved to New York City alone. How old was she? Where did she live? How did she find her way? She told me of winding roads and railroad tracks, loud horns and carfare. She taught me anything worth having was worth working hard for. With dedication and hard work come struggles and blessings. She enjoyed telling her stories. I only wish I had a tape recorder to listen to her now.

I would sit and wait all day, watching game shows and The Facts of

Life. The condo had an open concept, center island in the kitchen, large bay windows, a wraparound terrace, and a sitting room off to the side. I was not allowed to play with the onyx and alabaster chess set. I understood someone had a game going. To the left was a library and a globe set by the window. I was always flabbergasted that there was no TV in their bedroom.

My Gaga folded their clothes with precision. I helped. I was truly awestruck at the food in the refrigerator, multiples of everything, bottles of Perrier, and fruit I had never seen. It was so neatly organized with loads of healthy options. Seeing what you could have I knew growing up I had to have a pantry, walk-in closet, and extra space between the furniture.

My Gaga inspires me daily to exceed my yesteryears, prepare for my future, and ground myself in gratitude. May she continue to watch over my family with the rest of the ancestors who surround me.

With both boys growing and grown, I want so much for them. What about me? Lost—in a whirlwind of years. Stuck—in thoughts and no action. Comfortable yet grateful—for everything. I made a decision to challenge myself to use this time for metamorphosis. Even though I have what I need, I know I'm destined for more. I know that if I get uncomfortable, and get comfortable with being uncomfortable, I could be living the life of my dreams. Within these four walls so eloquently designed, I still visualize a space much greater. My windows could survey the mountains and the ocean, I could look over the valleys with the treetops, wildlife, and weather.

I close my eyes and sit quietly.

2033

I'm in Southern California. I have a home built in the Hills with floor-to-ceiling windows overlooking the ocean, the valley, and the mountains. A Fuji white Range Rover Velar, a bright white Wrangler Rubicon 4xe with 33-inch tires, and the "frog-eyed" Bentley Continental GT Sport in Old English white decorate my driveway. The two-story glass house has a pool, guest house, and a lush, manicured garden several hundred feet to the road. My driveway curves and empties at a 75-degree angle. As you walk in, you smell freshly baked cookies. The front entrance reveals the curved staircase and Gustav Klimt's The Kiss painted on the wall. The furniture is off-white with wooden accents and leather pillows thrown about. There's a treadmill in the living room and adjacent to the mural, in the corner, is a Harley-Davidson Sportster. The 40-inch television is mounted above the built-in bench and eat-in nook. The gourmet kitchen has white granite countertops waterfalling from the center island with state-of-the-art chrome appliances.

There's a long hallway that leads to the back. Grand paintings fill the walls. As you reach the end of the corridor it overlooks the most breathtaking view I could find. I sit there most mornings on the plush hammock and a jasmine fur throw to enjoy the breeze on my face. My personal chef comes in with my favorite: oatmeal chocolate chip. I deeply inhale the aroma before touching the warm, soft cookies. There are several aids to assist me in keeping the house and my affairs in order. The chauffeur and my assistant make sure I'm timely and my chef and trainer keep me tight.

I am next to the most loving, respectful, and generous man of my dreams, so handsome and in love with me. His eyes sparkle: they are the color of cinnamon fudge swirl. He has soft, full lips that he moistens before we kiss. He makes me laugh and giggle every time he's around. I finally feel secure in another person's arms, so strong and well-developed, with so much melanin he glistens in the sun.

I hear India.Arie singing, "I am ready for love with all the joy and the pain/ I will be patient, kind, faithful, honest, and true/ to a man who loves music/ a man who loves art/ respects the spirit world/ and thinks with his heart..."

He chews with his mouth open and grins, piercing me with his eyes. I am reminded of what a beautiful soul I've connected with. To share peace, space, and time. I finish folding the laundry and go to take his plate. He stops me and grabs me to sit down on his lap. I laugh and giggle as we kiss. He says he has something to ask me and needs my full attention. I blink hard to stare at his pupils to watch them dilate as he clears his throat. I feel his heart and I slow my breathing to match his. He smiles again. I'm pretty sure I know what he's going to ask. I close my eyes as the waiting is unbearable.

I love every second and relish in this moment, grateful to receive my present.

I finish breathing deeply and open my eyes.

January 13th, 2021

Forty-fifth President Donald J. Trump is impeached by the US House of Representatives for inciting a riot. It is the first time in history that a US President has been impeached twice. (18)

January 20th

Joe Biden is inaugurated as the 46th President of the United States of America and Kamala Harris as the 49th Vice President. The first Black, the first South Asian, and the first woman. Amanda Gorman recites, "The Hill We Climb." Previous office holder Donald Trump is the first outgoing President to refuse to attend the inauguration of his successor since 1869.

January 22nd

Is it ever okay to sit back and congratulate yourself? To bask in the sunshine?

To dance with pure joy and glee? To admire yourself and your possessions and be pleased? Happy. Is it okay to be happy? To smile. To take it all in, to enjoy, to truly feel peace. Is it okay? Without the crippling afterthoughts that it might all be taken away? Without the whispers? Without the doubt? To truly be happy—continuously and on a regular basis. To be free to look at yourself and smile from the inside?

Happy? Is it okay to be happy? Without...without explaining why? Why are you smiling? What are you laughing about? Why are you so happy?

Why you?

Why not me? My face, my name, my love, my karma, my realness, my rawness, my worth, my joy, my freedom, my peace, my song, my journey...

Haven't I been through enough? To finally feel joy. I am worthy of Joy. I am at peace.

I am Grateful. I am Worthy. I Matter, no? Well, let me say it again. I am Worthy, Trustworthy, and Lovable. I am more than enough.

Enough is enough...earliest memories: Watching the first man I ever loved beat Mommy. "It's all going to be okay, baby..." By age five, our divorce.

My name alone made children giggle and sing Sesame Street, "Sunny Days sweeping the clouds away" -every time I walked into a classroom. Every day, I would go home crying to Mommy, "Why did you name me— Sunny?"

I grew up with an older sister who acted as if she despised me simply because I was the tag along. (If she could've spit she would've. Somedays, she would purposefully talk to my forehead and just let her anger be felt with fresh spittle.) Pre-teens were my "Brace Face'" years, "When's the train coming?" years, and "I can't kiss you; you'll scratch my lips all up" years. Somewhere, I had mustered up enough confidence to audition for LaGuardia High School. I'm finally given accolades for standing out and making people notice. My sister's friends thought I was funny and asked for me to join them. Thankfully, by this time, she had stopped rolling her eyes at the sound of my name.

By age eighteen and after graduation, the family moved to Linwood, North Carolina. I took the change in environment as an excuse to abandon my immediate desire to act on stage. I equated Linwood to death. So, I went to cosmetology school instead of living my dream since it, too, was a natural gift. After two years in rural America, we moved back to the Big Apple with my 5-speed coupe. Too fast for my own damn good. I always skirted on the side of danger and the fast lane. I took my life as a joke and loved the feeling of a man more than I loved myself. I didn't know what to do so I decided to live by the seat of my pants.

At a pivotal moment in my life, I was hired at Vidal Sassoon on 5th Avenue (as an assistant) and at the same time chosen to direct the youth group at my local community theater company (as a volunteer). Both required a Saturday commitment; I couldn't imagine turning down the chance of working on 5th Avenue.

By twenty-five, I met the man who would change me. He showed me his "crazy", and I quelled mine. After years together, we had two sons. I never asked if he wanted children and then watched his mental breakdown. I stroked his back and said, "Baby, everything's going to be okay," too many times, which enraged him. He challenged my mental health with emotional and financial torture. I remember thinking, I gotta get out of here, but how? too many times. I allowed him nine years of my life with five fiercely unhappy. At thirty-four, I had to find peace for me and my boys. Being a single parent never sat well. My mental space spiraled downward as I moved back in with my mother. The rest of my thirties was a blur. I took the loss of my sister at a small, but winding degrade. Doctors and therapists saw to my prescribed happiness, shortly after the loss of my job at the unionized Verizon. (I sold Fios to their small business customers with great benefits and pension.)

My peace continued to be an issue with no end in sight. A year later I lost my apartment. I was forced to move back in again with my mother. Cue, age nine, hospitalized in ICU for weeks and now has a lifetime Cardiologist. Three years later, Thai was diagnosed with Epilepsy and now has a host of Neurologists. (The pharmacy and Express Scripts on speed dial 7 and 8.)

For Years… Undiagnosed Depression/PTSD/Attention Deficit Disorder/Anxiety mixed with Trauma Bonds only allowed me to oversleep, gain weight and verbally abuse myself while overusing pills, drugs and alcohol. I filled the void with sex as it felt natural. It was me. I was it. Really felt like nothing to give my body for a moment of solace.

By forty-seven, I actively pursue my demons to flush out the traumas. I stare my regrets in the eye and take stock in the choices that are mine. I acknowledge I was in a relationship with free will. I also know we both choose to make poor decisions from the beginning. Since I never felt enough, I needed a man's constant validation for just being around him. I learn slowly but highly advanced.

My life before 2020? Broken, but not destroyed. The glue used to mend the shards have flecks of gold in them. My hurt makes me unique, makes me, me. The rasp in my voice is deep and overqualified for the blues.

I use my journal as a reminder of growth and my own validity; I write therefore I am. I recall my journey as I try to understand my path, and chart for a new destination. With my energy and focus I am on my way.

Age 50: HERE I COME...Fierce and Fearless

I took a hiatus from reminiscing on specific details. Putting pen to paper revealed to me and anyone looking in, I needed help. There were certain dates and parties I did not want to immortalize. Therefore, therapy, self-reflection, and spiritual growth were past due.

Abraham Hicks once said, "And those who are watching this transformation will think you've suddenly become magical. They will want to know the magic wand you've found, and you will say to them, "I made peace with me. I stopped finding faults with me. I stopped finding faults in you. I stopped looking for reasons to feel bad and I started looking for reasons to feel good. I stopped making the worst of things and I started to make the best of things. I stopped asking other people to make me feel better and I decided I could be the reason I feel better. And in that decision, I found the ultimate freedom."

My life after the quarantine? There's only up from here. Embracing, "Sunny days ... sweeping the clouds away..."

April 8ᵗʰ

President Joe Biden says, "Gun violence in this country is an epidemic" as he unveils an executive package including restrictions on "ghost guns."

April 9th

DMX, 50, rapper and actor, loses his life after a drug overdose and heart attack. He was one of the most important figures of 2000s hip-hop. His lyrics vary from hardcore to prayer. He left his legacy with "What They Really Want" and "Party Up (Up in Here)." (19)

April 11th

Daunte Wright, 20, is shot and killed at a traffic stop because the officer mistakes their own gun for a taser in Brooklyn Center, Minnesota. (20)

April 14th

Ex-police officer Kim Potter is arrested and charged with second-degree manslaughter in the killing of Daunte Wright. (21)

April 20th

Ex-police officer Derek Chauvin is convicted of murdering George Floyd. (22)

According to the World Health Organization (WHO), a record 5.24 million COVID-19 cases are reported in one week. One third of those cases are in India.

May 19th

Comedian and writer Paul Mooney dies at 79. (23) His legendary comedic style should not be forgotten. Known for being "too real," he was the first Black person in the Writers Guild of America.

After 423 days of COVID-19 lockdown, New York City begins to reopen. The estimated death toll is 33,000. (24)

Thai continued to get in trouble for smoking in and around the school and was recommended for a drug program. I was partly to blame, so I sympathized with him. I, in turn, went through the system too. I needed to stop what I was doing so he could have a positive example at home. We went to the meetings together. I even had support from other parents going through similar situations. I recall the first night at AA; the speaker apologized to her mother and family and broke down in front of the huddle. I was touched. I never heard myself say, "I am an alcoholic." It was eye-opening. I caught a tear and knew my mother needed an apology as well.

I realized I had a problem. I am an alcoholic, I am an avid drug user, I am a sex addict. As two teenage sons were growing, closely watching me and beginning to question my choices. There were times they were more interested in my well-being than I was. On more than one occasion I remember leaving them in the car to go to the liquor store, getting drunk, and falling over. My mother had to take them away one morning because I was too drunk to care for them.

Hello, my name is Sunny. I am a recovering alcoholic. I have a problem. I choose, every day, to be better.

Juneteenth

President Joe Biden signed a bill passed by Congress to make this day a holiday. It will forever commentate the day the slaves learned they were free. Our Independence Day

The next week, I stood up to confess and cleanse my soul. I replayed the highlights of my life and felt shame for laughing off the pain and strife I caused. Shakespeare wrote, "To thine own self be true." Was I walking in my purpose or feeding the angry wolf inside? I hugged a few who heard me and could only sense what I was going through. I also extended an apology to Thai who hid his face while I spoke. It only deepened our bond.

June 25th

Derek Chauvin is sentenced to 22 years and 6 months for the murder of George Floyd. (25)

August 6th

I was forced to get the vaccine. I needed to air travel to Parris Island, South Carolina for Cue's Boot Camp graduation. I chose Johnson & Johnson. I appreciated it for its simplicity. My thought of getting Corona was, "Eh, if it hadn't happened in all this time..."

Congratulations Private First Class Zimmons of Platoon 1845!

August 24th

Kathy Hochul becomes the first female Governor of New York after Andrew Cuomo resigns over his sex scandal.

September 6th

Actor Michael Kenneth Williams, best known as Omar Little on The Wire, dies at 55 from fentanyl-laced heroin. (26) He is quoted, "Do me one favor. Don't be like me, be better than me. Stand on these shoulders and take it higher."

September 8th

The large statue of Confederate general Robert E. Lee is removed from Richmond, Virginia. (27)

September 9th, 2021

Ma, my mother's mother left us early Thursday morning at the age of 94. I remember just the week before, I kissed her neck as she quickly pinched her chin to her shoulder. I smiled as she giggled. Rest well, Ma.

September 11th

President Joe Biden and former Presidents Barack Obama and Bill Clinton come together in New York City to dedicate the 20th Anniversary of 9/11. (28)

September 17th

Squid Game frenzy made everyone run to Netflix; we fell right in line.

October 14th

Danielle, my work bestie, came over to my apartment to hangout for a while. Since it was her first time there, she looked around and was impressed with the layout. She enjoyed my embellishments, and asked questions about certain pieces. She gravitated to one of my artworks and inquired how it was constructed.

I had been enamored with the visual of my girl, Missy "Misdemeanor" Elliot, on the August 2019 cover of Marie Claire. I needed to frame it. I took a canvas of similar size and flipped it over. The magazine fit in and leveled with the wooden frame, making it appear extravagant. There was space in between the two which I filled with fish tank gravel. After it was glued into place, I painted the top half the same color as the background: sky blue. Missy's suit jacket is embroidered gold, black, and burnt orange; I smudged the white letters to enlarge the cover title. To set it all off, I blow-dried it in plastic cling wrap. Where it sits on my front mantle, it appears Missy is praying for you with her diamond-encrusted ICON medallion, my all-time favorite.

Another piece that caught her attention is not mine. I bought and love this artwork because it has the street numbers of my first address – 1343. I re-conceptualized it. In the original, the woman was pale, and it lacked color, the street signs were red, and the taxicab was in black and white. Once I got it home and I painted over the areas that needed my flair but many of the three-dimensional accents of the original still shine through. Now the New York City sky-scape pops with a little more color, style, and authenticity. Still with the train station, deli, one way sign, and the skyscrapers and buildings in the back with metal and bolts on its rough wooden canvas; It stands out.

Danielle and I always laugh together. I call her my "mini-me" because she just turned thirty and reminds me of me—the pale blonde version. We have similar interests in men and enjoy the hood bars together. If it wasn't for her, I would forget to wear lashes. I love her dedication to the daily strips. We both smoke and enjoy making fun of our co-workers. We bonded that night when we realized we both had absent fathers except for hers lived in the house.

Once in the kitchen to get a snack, she observed the two boxes of General Mills Wheaties sitting in the corner. Her first reaction was, "Eww! You eat Wheaties?!"

I chuckled. "No, they're collectables."

On the right, the box is from 2001 with Serena Williams screaming in victory. On the left, is from 2020 which features LeBron James on the front and the back displays his I Promise School. These are mere cereal boxes to some but to me, they signify how far we've come.

I explained, "When I was growing up in the 70s and 80s, there was only Bruce Jenner, Mary Lou Retton, Chris Evert, Pete Rose, Larry Bird, and Babe Ruth on the cover. We were all overjoyed when Walter Payton made it to the cereal box in the late 80s." It was considered "the place to be" when given the endorsement deal by "the Breakfast of Champions."

I let her know, "We don't eat Wheaties. We celebrate Black Excellence."

November 2nd

Former police captain Eric Adams is elected New York City Mayor; he's the second Black mayor after David Dinkins (1990-1993). (29)

November 28th

Virgil Abloh, former CEO at Off White, was the first African to hold the position as Artistic Director for Louis Vuitton. (30) He died at the age 41 in Chicago. Louis Vuitton remembers him with a collection entitled, "Virgil was Here."

December

Rihanna's Savage X Fenty Named Most Influential Company of 2021

HAPPY NEW YEAR!

January 6th, 2022

Sidney Poitier, the first Black actor to win the Oscar for Best Actor, will be sorely missed at the age of 94. (31)

January 17th

Joel Osteen spoke to me through YouTube: "I want to talk to you about A New Mindset. It's easy to get stuck in life and think that we've gone as far as we can; we can't break the addiction, we can't get well, we'll never accomplish that dream. What's holding us back is our own thinking. Jesus said, "You can't put wine in old wineskins." Then Joel tells the story of when they used to use leather as a wine bottle, and it would wither after consumption. You couldn't use it again; you would have to get a new.

He continues, "You can't have a new life with old thinking." If you think you've reached your limit, then you have. If you think the problem is too big, then it is. If you think you'll never meet the right person, you probably won't. It's not that God doesn't have blessings, favor, increase- is that your skin is old? ... You have to get a new mindset. Start believing bigger, dreaming bigger, expecting bigger.

You're not limited by your circumstances, by the pandemic, by your boss, by how you were raised. One touch of God's favor will catapult you ahead. "God, I don't see a way, but I know you have a way. The medical report doesn't look good, but I know you're a Healer. I'm struggling with my finances, but I believe abundance is coming. This dream looks impossible, but I know you can open doors that no person can shut."

Joel then goes on to tell the story, from Acts chapter 3, of a crippled man begging with a cup wanting a few coins. Peter and John walk by and instead of giving to the man John tells him to walk. Since no one else ever spoke faith over him he was confused. John pulls him up, he drops his cup, and he walks.

"God is saying get rid of your cup. The blessing he has for you cannot be contained in a cup. As long as you have a "cup mentality" you'll be sitting at the gate thinking you're stuck at the mercy of other people. Hoping someone will give you a break, you don't need people. Yes, God will use people, but people are not your source. Quit looking for your cousin, your neighbor, your friend, your pastor and start looking to God. People are limited, God is unlimited. People can give you a short-term fix, but God can take you from being crippled to walking, from borrowing to lending, from addiction to freedom, from sickness to health, from lack to abundance.

God has sent me today to pull you up, quit making excuses, quit coming up with reasons why you can't be successful, can't be well, can't live free, can't get married, can't go to the next level. Get rid of that cup, you weren't created to just get a few coins here and there, survive, make it through. What God is going to do in your life will not fit in a cup. You may be limited but God is unlimited. He's about to do something that you've never seen. The scripture says he will open the windows of heaven and pour out blessings that cannot be contained in that cup. God wants to show you surpassing greatness of his favor. Don't go into a new year with low expectations, have a bigger vision, get your hopes up, you have to give God permission to bless you." (32)

January 21st

It hit me. It was a lethargic feeling I had never felt before. Light and standing hurt. All day I required my bed and nothing else mattered. I sneezed a couple times, coughed with hard, deep breaths; I couldn't even look at my phone. I didn't want to consider it, but for the next few days, if I mentioned to someone that I felt sick, the immediate response was, "Did you test yourself? You should get tested." I didn't have the strength.

After sleeping for seventeen hours, eating something, and then going back to bed, I felt myself again. Was it a 36-hour "flu"? To this day, I still don't know, but thanks, J&J!

Worst birthday ever. Thanks, COVID!

February 3rd

While watching episode five Inventing Anna on Netflix, I saw a familiar face. It was Michael, my classmate from LAG. Laughing out loud, I text him "Congratulations! (Kissy Face Emoji)" I admire him for keeping the dream alive and for being a continuous motivating force.

He texted back, "Thanks love! You're next!"

I looked around with an inquisitive stare. Me?

I turned my attention back to the series. My new love interest: Laverne Cox.

March 25th

Season two of Bridgerton breaks records with viewership surpassing the first. (33) The series is renewed for a third and fourth season. My British needs work.

March 27th

Mental health scare heard around the world. Will Smith has to apologize for his actions live on the Oscar stage.

April 17th

New York City's Hot 97 DJ Kay Slay loses his battle with COVID-19 at the age of 55. (34)

May 13th

Welcome to the world, RZA Athelston Mayers. (35) Rihanna and A$AP

Rocky released the name of their son nearly a year following his birth. His namesake is rapper and producer RZA, founding member of the Wu-Tang Clan (Wu-Tang is for the children).

June 16th

Thai graduated from Westfield High School. Fortunately, he and his class got to walk across the stage.

Congratulations Class of 2022!

Happy Juneteenth!

June 30rd

Honorable Ketanji Brown Jackson is sworn in as the first Black woman in the Supreme Court. (36)

July 3rd

In the perpetual state of single dumbfuckness, I am not where I want to be, but I am content and saddened at the same time. Can't complain but want growth. It feels like one step forward two steps back or one step and seventeen back. And it's all my call, my decisions, my doing and my give-a-fuckless behavior that hasn't been serving me. So therein lies the issue, nothing changes if we don't change. My therapist encourages me to see, "...real growth happens in small increments. Building on daily habits."

During today's doctor's visit, I was told I have Type 2 diabetes and was prescribed Metformin. Along with the diagnosis, I was advised to cut down on eating rice, bread, pasta, potatoes, and sugar. The doctor suggested an appointment in two months to retake the blood work and reevaluate my situation. I walked away with a chuckle, "That's almost everything."

July 7th

The National Football League hired their first black female president, Sandra Douglass Morgan, to run the Las Vegas Raiders. (37)

11:16PM

"MA!" Thai called from the living room.

"WHAT!" I moved quickly to the door.

He was standing outside my room, pointing up. "Did you just hear THAT!?"

Standing quietly, I shook my head and listened. "No, what was it?"

Thai was visibly shaken. "Someone upstairs just fell..." He pointed to the ceiling again. "She sounded—You didn't hear that?"

I was perplexed. I wanted to hear what he heard, so we stood for a second or two until we realized the noise had stopped. We were about to brush it off and assume she just fell when, above our heads, the noise exploded again. We heard a loud thud, a whimper, then a man's voice. Feet rushing. We followed the sounds and asked each other, what should we do?

It was abrupt; it startled Thai. He was upset and confused. Thai wanted to help his neighbor. She called out for help. She said no. What could be done? Stand by and watch, charge up there and suggest serious life changes, or call 911?

As the noise above our heads weirdly stopped, Thai and I sat on the couch where he voiced his concerns. Unfortunately, I was left with the daunting task of informing my offspring that people choose to live their lives and pay extra for privacy. And sometimes, you have to mind your business; but then there is also a line, which is blurry, where the law is needed. I was torn up inside that I had to teach the protocol for overhearing someone in distress in their own safe haven.

We didn't call for immediate intervention. In turn we agreed to write a quick note saying hello and attached the number of the New Jersey Domestic Violence Hotline. The information inside the packet matched what I was sent home with years before. I thought of how quickly she might dismiss any piece of paper we put on her doorstep to suggest things were out of control. We run the risk of being told to mind our business but as citizens of the world for peace and unity, I would only hope that if I cried out for help, someone would help me.

August 8th

The Office of Public Affairs published:

A federal judge in the Southern District of Georgia today sentenced Travis McMichael, 36, to life plus 10 years in prison; and his father Gregory McMichael, 66, to life plus seven years in prison; and William "Roddie" Bryan, 52, to 35 years in prison, for committing federal hate crimes and other offenses and connection with the killing of Ahmaud Arbery, a young black man, who was jogging in on public streets of a Brunswick neighborhood when he was chased down and shot to death in February 2020.

August 17th

I took stock of how much sugar and bread I put into my mouth on a daily basis. Iced tea, soda, burger and fries, pizza, chips, potato salad, donuts, cookies, cake, and bagels with cream cheese. Five Guys, Burger King, Popeye's, Shake Shack, McDonald's, Wendy's, Starbucks and Dunkin'. I knew all of that would have to come to an end. My upcoming appointment was in less than a month. I made myself crave water with lemon. Gave myself a half-a-gallon water challenge, I bought more fruit and displayed it on the counter. I made meatless Mondays a thing, packed my lunch, and started eating corn on the cob, more broccoli, and beans without the rice.

That same month, I rescued a dog. We kept his name, Winslow. He is God-sent, a mini pincher from Texas. We drove to Connecticut to pick him up. In all honesty, I hadn't walked outside in years. I instantly fell in love and, with so much energy, I challenged myself to walk him further. I met my neighbors, charted the distance around town, and became a believer in small miracles. Winslow was just what I needed to get out of the house and stop and smell the roses, watch the birds, chase the leaves, and laugh. He lived in every moment and demanded that I enjoy the view.

By my next doctor's visit, I had lost 37 pounds. He asked, "What have you been doing?" I credited Winslow, "I love your dog. Keep up the good work." I knew most of the weight I can contribute from eliminating alcohol from my weekends. I thanked him and continued my forward trajectory.

November 1st, 2022

Aunt Valerie left us too soon. She did leave us with lessons on self-care. Just two weeks ago, I called her and told her I bought a dog and she said, "Oh! You got money." One of her favorite sayings. She still makes me laugh.

CHAPTER NINE

HAPPY NEW YEAR!

January 22nd, 2023

HBD! For my 50th—an affair to be remembered. The invite spoke of discreet fun with a masquerade ball theme. The invite was a mini-NDA that you uploaded to your phone and needed to acknowledge before giving further details. No one not invited could attend. No pictures with location, no tags, and no sharing what just went down. The location was the rooftop of my building. Black and white balloons filled the corners with little LEDs in them illuminating the night sky. The weather was cool and brisk. I wore a flowing white off the shoulder gown with black roses. The thigh-high black boots and long black gloves accentuated my simple black mask. Under my dress hid my belly dancing hip sash. The Master of Ceremony announced my arrival and my circle of friends, family, and extended cheered for me and in that moment, I blushed for real and felt pure joy. I performed a small segment of a dance I perfected with a belly dancing drum beat. Every time I wiggled my hips the crowd roared with excitement. The chatter of the coins was a surprise and caused wonder filled eyes.

Two camping tents for six were used as hot boxes. (Hot box: when there's no ventilation for the smoke to escape.) Weed-ish Fish, Stoners Patch, Starbuds Gummies, and other edibles covered the tables along with a few pre-rolls. Bring Your Own B- meant a few different things at this event (Bud or Bottle take your pick). Less than twenty people made it out but the DJ read the crowd and kept Burna Boy, Davido, Sleepy Hallow, and Polo G on guaranteed rotation. It was a night to be remembered—but that's all I can say about that.

January 23rd

Five ex-Memphis police officers are charged with murdering Tyre Nichols who they beat at a traffic stop on January 7th. Memphis Councilman Martavius Jones breaks down in tears with Don Lemon on CNN. He says, "It wasn't supposed to end like this." (38)

Take the Black Man Out Your Scope (A Poem)

Put your Second Amendment right down for a minute, to see the black man is always in your crosshairs. Stop pulling the trigger, put the gun down. The black man is under attack. Take your foot off his back, let him up out of prison and give him his 13th Amendment back. Let's talk about the generational wealth gap, police men killing us back-to-back. Karen with her latest iPhone trying to destroy the black man's vibe, and now "this man's president perpetrating the whitewashed lie. Saying he's going to Make America Great...again?

We need your help to see how His-story has held "us" back. It's time to give the black man white man privilege. Treat him like your neighbor, your doctor, your business associate.

See the black man as your friend, your brother, as a human on this earth at the same time and place for a reason. If you are a child of God, all beings matter without question.

It's easy for me to see, just take the black man out your scope.

DROP YOUR WEAPON, OFFICER. (Hands up.) DON'T SHOOT!

February 12th

Rihanna graced Super Bowl LVII in a stunning red ensemble fit for a queen as her baby bump made its debut.

Rest in Peace to Dave Trugoy the Dove from De La Soul. De La Soul is from the Soul. (40)

February 14th

Musician and rapper Pharrell Williams is appointed menswear designer for Louis Vuitton. (41)

March 17th

Actor and musician Lance Reddick dies at the age of 60 due to heart disease. He was best known for his work in The Wire and the John Wick series.

(42)

March 30th

Former US President Trump is indicted by a Manhattan grand jury over payments to porn star Stormy Daniels. He's the first US President to face criminal charges. *(43)*

Benjamin texted me. Tiffany and him broke up and he wondered if I'd like to come over and smoke.

Benjamin

> Wow, hope she's doing alright...

Did you wanna come over?

> Nah, we good (Block/Delete)

April 14th

I get in deep with Ali Wong and Beef on Netflix.

April 25th

Legendary singer, activist, and actor Harry Belafonte dies in his Manhattan home. He was 96. (44)

May 3rd

Missy "Misdemeanor" Elliott is inducted into the Rock and Roll Hall of Fame. (45)

May 4th

COVID-19 is no longer a global health emergency issued by The World Health Organization. Even though it remains a significant threat. The world wide's death toll is approximately 20 million.

May 9th

Former US President Trump is found guilty of sexually abusing E. Jean Carroll in a New York court and ordered to pay $5 million for battery and defamation. (46)

I was watching Netflix, I was watching Hulu, I was watching Prime. I saw a documentary about a woman who got shot in the face by her husband. The story was horrific on so many different levels. Not only did she live to tell the details of how he shot her in the face, he did it in front of their children. She was able to crawl for help because the babies were small and, thankfully, not hurt. The program went off, and I couldn't get this woman and her before-and-after photos out of my mind. It jarred me out of my sleep; I was compelled to go to her GoFundMe page. I had full intentions of aiding her in any little way that I could, knowing from experience any pocket-sized bit helps. I forgot her name while going over to the computer. I googled the news channel and searched "mother shot in the face and lived." I was overwhelmed by how many stories came up. I could have chosen from dozens of women to donate to their GoFundMe. I then put, "Black mother shot in face," "Black mother shot in Detroit..." The list kept getting longer.

At that moment, I realized my situation could be a lot worse and I could be completely devastated. I understood that I was blessed. I was able to get away quickly and tell my story. And in some way, reach out to others in similar or way worse situations.

I decided against the gun and halted all tactical lessons. I didn't occupy that level of decency; I was not mentally sound enough. I was still working through issues that mandate I should not own a gun.

I envisioned myself at home with the new weapon. The first strange sound startles me awake. I am forced to go to the window. I attempt to see through the dark shadows. Behind the tree stands the enraged man who has promised to come get me. He looks over his shoulder and down the block. He crosses the street to approach my home. I think it was Friday the 13th because all I saw was Jason. I'm dumb-fucked as I feel every nerve in my spine, my heart triples speed, and then—what? He finishes what he started? Touches my family because they're trying to protect me? The thought sets my throat on fire—that someone could have the evilness inside of them to harm and go out of their way to make other people's lives unpleasant.

In my dream, I reach back to retrieve my loaded Sig Sauer 1-9-11, as the law permits, since he is within 1,000 feet from me and my home. I peer outside and get down on one knee to stabilize myself and take aim. I roar,

"You're not welcome here. The police are on their way. Leave now or I'll be forced to shoot your ass!" He looks like he has a long gun pressed against his thigh. His slow stride pulls the air from my lungs. I pull back the safety and, at the same time, put my finger on the trigger. I take joy as I curl my index finger in and look through the scope. I recall the officer telling me, "As long as he doesn't have his back to you," I'm within the legal right to kill this motherfucker.

BANG! The nightmare roused me from sleep. I sat with sweaty palms and took deep breaths. I rest better now knowing my sons are safe in their home. Without a gun, there are no potential "accidents."

May 18th

Roberta, 96, is rushed to the hospital for complaints of chest pains. She gets diagnosed with indigestion and heartburn. Due to her overall weakness, the rehab center finds her a home. Fortunately, Garnet is there to care for her.

I realized after months of visiting and shopping for her, her offer to give me her home was only an incentive to be there and care for her for the rest of her life. Unfortunately, the wounded little girl didn't accept her 40-year-old apology for allowing the divorce to separate us as she never asked for my return. May she live to be a hundred and seven.

May 24th

Tina Turner dies at 83. "Eat the cake, Anna Mae" was made famous by her abuser. Tina traveled the world regardless of him, performing her "What's Love Got to Do With it?" anthem. She will be sorely missed. (47)

Former U.S. Youth Poet Laureate Amanda Gorman's poem, "The Hill We Climb" is put on a restricted reading list at Bob Graham Education Center, Miami Lakes, amid increasing censorship in Florida.(48)

June 7th

New York's air quality sinks to the lowest in the world (air quality index 218) as smoke from Canadian wildfires blankets the American Northeast. (49)

Thai started a certificate program at the Fashion Institute of Technology. We went together so I could teach my suburban New Jersey-raised son; the route on the bus to the streets of grimy 42nd Street/Port Authority and then to the underbelly of the New York City train system. For the first time in his life, he would be traveling downtown to 27th Street, alone.

Lord, if you are watching, I need you now.

June 16th

Mom and I set sail to the Bahamas for seven days of adventure and overdue relaxation. (At the same time, Thai was navigating the #1 train somewhere in Manhattan.) The trip was a vacation for two, to commemorate Mom's 70th year on this Earth and her retirement from educating high school students about "sex, drugs and rock-n-roll." The first Black woman to teach at Ridgewood High School.

June 20th

Pharrell Williams is praised for his much-anticipated debut as Louis Vuitton's Creative Director on Tuesday. He debuts his beautiful six-year-old triplets for the first time as the family dons camouflage suits inspired by Minecraft.

June 26th

Don Lemon announces that he's been fired from CNN after seventeen years at the cable news network. The same day, Fox News anchor Tucker Carlson is ousted from the conservative network by Fox Corporation chairman Rupert Murdoch. (50)

July 7th

David Simon, co-creator of The Wire, asks for leniency for the man who sold Michael K. Williams a lethal dose of fentanyl. (51)

July/August 2023

Missy "Misdemeanor" Elliot radiates on the cover of Essence in a gold jumpsuit, enormous gold hoops, and big black boots. The cover reads: Missy's Midas Touch; The Supa Dupa Star's Road to THE ROCK & ROLL HALL OF FAME.

August 3rd

Magoo, best known for work with Timbaland and Missy, loses his life at age 50. (52)

Rihanna and A$AP Rocky welcome their second son, Riot Rose. (53)

August 5th

The day is now and will forever be a National Black Holiday for The Montgomery Riverboat Brawl. (54) This same riverfront once was one of the largest slave ports in the country. Montgomery, Alabama is the capital of the confederacy and once the center of white supremacy. This is the same Montgomery where John Lewis marched from Selma to end segregation and they bashed his skull in. The same Montgomery where they sent attack dogs and sprayed fire hoses on Black people who were protesting for civil rights, the same Montgomery which is known to bomb homes and churches with little children inside. (55) Say what you will about that day, but we feel like that ass whooping was well deserved and well overdue.

Best meme to put a visual spin on it was by Ellis and Eli on TikTok @liveprod "Black Avengers" 8-9 Hashtag Montgomery Brawl... Two white teenagers' film in their backyard with a pool talking about their boat. A black teenager appears pointing; an altercation ensues, and they scuffle. In slow motion, the black teenager throws his hat into the air, and it activates a call for Black Panther and Aquaman who swims through the pool. A smackdown ensues, and the two-go flying. Now one of the first teens is dressed as, what looks like, a woman; she gasps and "clutches pearls." A white folded chair slaps her across the face, twice then pushed in the pool. Funniest shit I've seen all day.

To commemorate, white fold-up chairs available at Walmart 2-for-$10.

August 9th

Simone Biles returns to dominate and cause an uproar on the American gymnastics team.

August 23rd

HAPPY 50th BIRTHDAY to HIP-HOP! I spent that Saturday in front of

1520 Sedgwick Avenue, the original birthplace of hip hop. "Up the Bronx, where the people are fresh"— the streets were lined with food trucks and the parks were filled with old heads and young ones vibing to the music. I heard KRS-One spit a few nostalgic ones, "The Bridge is Over" and "South Bronx." Bopped along with Slick Rick with "La Di Da Di," and threw my hands up with DJ Kool Herc on the ones and twos. People brought chairs and coolers and covered the sidewalk.

Sedgwick is a long, curved road about a mile long full of colorful characters, police, t-shirt vendors, and amplified hip hop sounds coming from every direction. The right side of the block looks over the northbound Major Deegan Expressway. At the end of the avenue a stage was set. I didn't want to sit too close to the stage, so we stayed back. With the amount of music lovers, I didn't see any performers but definitely heard them and enjoyed the day. The drone show capped the night off and captivated all in attendance. It felt like a few hundred sparklers in the sky. Hands down the best drone configuration was the breakdancer in slow motion and my second favorite had to be the hand dropping the mic.

Sunday, the streets of Harlem were filled with love and thumping bass. I scanned the crowd and noticed: music soothes the soul and uplifts. You could feel the music as the beat vibrated everyone in sync. All colors, from eggplant to cashew, showed out. All generations from diapers to bucket hats came to show when they first fell in love with Hip Hop.

I met a little one in a stroller and what looked like her Nana but found out it was her sitter. I had to take pictures to chronicle this time. She danced along and jumped to the beat. To this day, her parents have no clue their baby loves good music.

I was enjoying the flow and sang along, "Step into a World / Where there's no one left / But the very best / No MC can test / Step into a world, where hip-hop is me / Where MC's and DJ's / Build up their skills as they play every day / For the rapture/ Yes! Yes! Y'all ya don't stop/ KRS-One, Rock on! / Yes! Yes! Y'all ya don't stop/ KRS-One, Rock on!"

All five boroughs partied and celebrated Hip Hop. Events popped off all month long.

Friday night's concert at Yankee Stadium was streamed on YouTube the next day. Four hours was maybe too long for me, but they brought together talent old and new.

Some of my favorites: Dougie Fresh, Eric B and Rakim, Run DMC, Queen Latifah, LL Cool J, Special Ed, Nas, Busta Rhymes, MC Lyte, Das EFX, Onyx, Andre 3000 and Outkast, M.O.P, Mobb Deep, The Fugees, Young MA, Lil Wayne, J. Cole, Kendrick Lamar, Lil' Kim, Common, Red Man, Method Man and the Wu-Tang Clan, A Tribe Called Quest, Black Thought and The Roots, to name a few.

Notably missed are those lost to gun violence including Biggie in 1997, 2Pac in 1996, Jam Master Jay in 2002, Nipsey Hustle in 2019, Take Off 2022, Young Dolph 2021, XXXTentacion 2018. We also lost legends to accidental drug overdoses: DMX in 2022, Shock G in 2021, Ol'Dirty Bastard in 2004, Coolie 2022, Gangsta Boo 2023. We pour out a lil' liquor.

August 14th

From CNN: An Atlanta-based grand jury indicts Trump and eighteen others on state charges stemming from alleged efforts to overturn the former president's 2020 electoral defeat. The historic indictment is the fourth criminal case that Trump is facing. (56)

August 24th

Former US president Donald Trump surrenders at Fulton County Jail to be arrested on charges stemming from his attempts to alter the 2020 Georgia election. He gets a mugshot. (57)

August 31st

New York City proclaims this day, Biz Markie Day. A ceremony is held at Marcus Garvey Park Amphitheater. (58) Important to those who cherish hip-hop as a voice, a teacher and a lifestyle. Biz Markie pioneered beat boxing and made the music with his mouth. May future generations sit at the feet of their great grandparents and learn the lyrics and sing along, "Oh baby you/ got what I need/ but she say/'he's just a friend'/ but she say/ 'he's just a friend'." (59)

September 5th

From the Department of Justice: The leader of the Proud Boys is sentenced to twenty-two years in prison for seditious conspiracy and other charges related to the January 6th capitol breach. This is the longest sentence yet of those convicted.

September 6th

Ava DuVernay's film Origin is the first by an African American woman to compete at the Venice Film Festival. (60)

Still very heavy on IG, I tracked the comings and goings of people I felt like I knew.

I gawked at friends who braved the airports with masks, gloves, and coveralls. A few acquaintances stood out as nomad travelers, and I quietly envied them. My girl, Ayvette (Class of '91), seemingly stayed busy with travels to Dubai, Egypt, Jamaica, and Venezuela. Her beautifully manicured locs were long, past her shoulders. She had the new S-Class Mercedes in white. I'm not sure the year but, knowing Ayvette, it was a lease. She sells homes and owns her own business, mansion, and small fleet of cars in Atlanta.

I lived vicariously through her reels as she devoted herself to the gym. Longingly, I desired the same commitment. Watched her daily workout posts—she'd lost a commendable amount of weight. I liked most of her vids except for when it seemed like too much. Part-time hater? Or true friend? I shook my head and forced myself to "heart" one of the new ones where she was squatting with a trainer waving the weighted ropes. I didn't love it; I was more concerned her back muscles would be as big as her head.

I spotted an IG caption which was different from the rest. She posted: "Check on Your Strong Friends, Too." A few hours went by before I imagined she may be alluding to herself. I texted, "Hey! How are u?" She texted that she was fine. We wrote back and forth and promised to get together soon. We hadn't spoken since Cue's graduation last year.

Ayvette and I go back, like snow cones and Cabbage Patch dolls with the new Trapper Keepers. We went to the same art-based primary school in Spanish Harlem for fifth and sixth grade. We reunited in high school over our love for drama. I recall her and I doing a scene from The Women of Brewster Place written by Gloria Naylor.

We played a lesbian couple who lived on Brewster Place. My character, Lorraine, starts the scene by walking in carrying groceries. She voiced her concern about the neighbors and said something like, "They said we should be ashamed...they said..." The most prominent line I do remember was when Ayvette's character, Theresa, asked, "Who's 'they'?"

My best friend Maryam, Ayvette and I would travel home together since we all lived in Southside Jamaica, Queens. Ayvette stands out in my memory as being privileged or loved by both parents. Her family owned a cleaning business and it quickly gained buzz. Her mother was acknowledged for her achievements and work in the community. Her image was captured on a subway poster along with her accolades. Every day after school, we would walk through 179th Street station and see her mom. "I love to hear the story again and again how it all got started way back when..." (61), her words and her stories. Her stories and her words were boastful and proud.

Last Friday night, Ayvette appeared in my dream. It was a party, grand, and she hosted. I was amongst others waiting outside; she waved me in and whispered to the doorman. Feathers, cocktails, and bowties. It was obvious the crowd was there to celebrate her. I remember laughing and talking with her. Toward the end of the night, she pulled me aside and said she wanted me to meet someone, her husband. I followed her and wondered where he'd been all night. She escorted me into a room; it was sleepy but somehow upbeat. Just a few people were there which made me excited; I was one of them! Her husband was seated. I can't recall his face; I do remember him being older and dressed in a suit and leather loafers. She introduced me and explained they appreciated a polyamorous relationship, and she would be delighted to watch me, and her husband enjoy foreplay. I don't recall my immediate answer, but as the dream continued, I moved to another room with another couple and her husband. They all just seemed too old for me, and as I looked over my shoulder, Ayvette was there watching. I was confused and scared. Was this how she lived? Is this how she dressed so beautifully and drove fabulous cars? Was she a "kept woman"?

When I woke up, I was baffled. Was I having a premonition or was this just a mere fantasy?

September 9th

Coco Gauff vanquishes her opponents at the US Open, glowing so bright right now.

September 11th

May we never forget 9/11.

The US economy stimulated a stunning 8.5-billion-dollar growth due to Barbie, and Oppenheimer opening at the box office, as well as tours featuring Beyonce and Taylor Swift. According to Morgan Stanley. Variety

September 12th

Cardi B and Megan Thee Stallion perform their new song "Bongos" at the Video Music Awards. Taylor Swift sweeps the award show with nine statues. Rema makes it to the world stage with his song, "Calm Down" with Selena Gomez, and wins—a first for Afrobeats.

September 14th

Hunter Biden, son of US President Joe Biden, is indicted on charges tied to the possession of a gun while using narcotics. (62)

September 15th, 2023

The day marks 60 years since the KKK bombed an Alabama church, murdering four little black girls. Addie May Collins, born April 18, 1949; Carol Denise McNair, November 17, 1951; Carole Rosamond Robertson, April 24, 1949; and Cynthia Diane Wesley, April 30, 1949. A fifth girl lived to tell the story: Sarah Collins Rudolph, Addie's sister. We shall never forget.

September 18th

Sha'Carri Richardson floats in her natural hair as she breaks records as the fastest woman in the world. (63) And is it just me? Or are all the gold and silver medalists in track and field black women?

Fashion journalist Chioma Nnadi is named the new head of British Vogue. She's the first Black woman to head a major fashion magazine. (64)

Our new mantra is "Support Black Owned Businesses" to "Bank Black" and "Support Black Owned Brands." The love in the people is evident, the culture is always adored and the overall admiration in one's community is renewed and given a whole new flex. "Black and brown people" are a force to reckoned with and it highlights the conversation; If you win, I win and if I win, we all win.

September 23rd

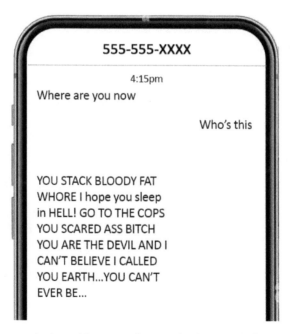

As I read his words, I could see, underneath, the sender's true message.

555-555-XXXX

I AM SMALL AND HAVE NOT
GROWN PAST WHERE YOU
LEFT ME. I THINK OF YOU
AND I HURT FROM PAST
TRAUMAS I HAVEN'T
HEALED AND I WANT TO
TAKE MY ANGER FRUSTRA-
TION OUT ON YOU. I WANT
SOME PIECE OF YOU TO
HOLD ON TO...I'VE BEEN
SENT HERE TO DERAIL
YOUR PROGRESS TO LEAVE
YOU IN TRAUMA PIECES
AND HOPEFULLY DIMINISH
YOUR SHINE I AM NOT
ENOUGH I'M A WEAK
LITTLE MAN AND
TERRORIZING YOU MAKES
FEEL STRONG AND
IMPORTANT IN A
DEMENTED AND FUCKED
UP KIND OF WAY
BLAH-BA-DI-BLAH-BLAH
Blah-do-do-di-do-doo-doo-
poo-poo

Nigga! It's been four
years Let that shit go.
(Block and Delete)

CHAPTER TEN

Joy and pain, sunshine, and rain.

Sunshine, a nickname I adopted from the Manhattan salon on the upper West Side. I channel Dandridge because she was also beautiful and talented. People also attempted to break her spirit. She was born in the 20s and enjoyed performing on stage and film. Her most notable film: Carmen Jones, where she was nominated for an Academy Award for Best Actress and the first Black woman to do so. Halle Berry portrayed her in HBO's film, Introducing Dorothy Dandridge. She is remembered for demanding to be treated equally and one of the first Black women to be portrayed as more than just a maid or servant.

I was born on the 20th floor of Mount Sinai Hospital in Manhattan and brought to the Bronx in 1973 to live. The birth year and birthplace of Hip Hop. Standing at about five foot six, 195 pounds, I am voluptuous, heavy-chested, but no ass at all. I am cafe con leche light skin—the complexion most white people envy. They see me as the ultimate tan, not too dark and non-white.

Sometimes when enjoying the poolside amenities of my apartment complex, I reflect and smile because Dorothy and other little Black girls couldn't even dip their toe in pools like this. My joy is so her pain will never go unrecognized.

On my IG page, there are pictures of me absolutely loving myself, feeling my curves and all my edges. The pictures are nothing more or nothing less than I want you to see. Natural to no makeup, dewy skin, and a head full of highlighted locs I skillfully cut into an asymmetrical bob which now grazes my shoulders. My pics showcase me during my travels around town, local rallies, house parties; they are more intimate than grand. Most, to all, of my images are me smiling and dancing or sitting pretty with a coy grin.

May 12th

Shine

Shine	*even when your throat hurt and nobody's listening.*
Shine	*while you are washing the dishes back in the kitchen.*
Shine	*like you broke. Now what?*
Shine	*when your throat hurt and ain't nobody lying, hurting, or stealing.*
Shine	*when you done smoke and finished hope.*
Shine	*like you are here for reason and got something to say.*
Shine	*cuz your constant struggle is getting OUT-OF-COMFORT*
Shine	*even when you really don't want to...just shine.*

After four years, I felt a calling back to Facebook. I'm glad I did. I reconnected with LAG and realized I missed my friends. Luckily, I was in time for a reunion hosted by the class of '88. They extended the invite to all classes. We had a memorable night at Bodega 88. The establishment flowed out into the street cafe. After COVID-19, restaurants and bars set up tables taking up valuable parking spots but allowing people to get together. Vanessa and her man opened his bar for the affair. She's a fellow poet and was promoting her stage show, A Gay and a Jew Walk Into a Bar: A comedy.

T'rah was there, who I've always looked up to. She's impressed me with her style and grace. She's still divine and an MUA for models on the runway. Model and full-figured showstopper, Tonya made an appearance. She always makes me laugh. We took selfies. She alluded that she's working on a reality show; I liked to see that. She's my FB fashion guru with pictures of the celebrities as they're stepping off the red carpet.

Tasha and her husband, Zachery, are first-class and famous in my eyes. Her party a few years ago still inspires me to rent out a club with a band with me on the mic. Tina, who I hadn't seen since high school, brought back teenage memories. We exchanged info and promised not to let more time pass. So many people made it out. I only knew a handful; most I connected with later.

Tara, my ace-boon-coon, came late as usual, but just in time to take pictures with Pilar, the published illustrator. If I would've known Pilar was coming, I would've bought her book, so she could've signed it for me.

Tara and I bonded after our first reunion party 15 years ago, when the after-party was at a 24-hour diner for breakfast. Our four children have grown together. I thank her, too, for being a constant positive force in my life. We posted our pictures to Facebook so others who didn't attend could envy the perfect night with old friends, drinks, and the outdoors.

The next day, someone from the class of '91 posted Trump's mugshot with the caption: "WANTED FOR PRESIDENT 2024!" Is this a joke? Same thing I asked when he ran the first time.

After shaking my head, I was delighted to hear that an off-Broadway production of "I Am Relentless", a one-woman show was coming to Theatre's Row soon. Written and performed by class of '91, Reishon "Staxx" Cordero. She invited her FB page to come celebrate her 50th birthday by loving her life on stage. "I Am Relentless" in bookstores and movie with the same title on Tubi.

I invited Danielle. We sat in the second row and giggled as the show started. Reishon moved through her youth with voices. Her baby voice needed more concentration. Her dad's and nana's voices were spot-on, and her voice rang out. In her nana's memories, she handed out hard candies to the front row. Almost seemed as if she spoke to the audience and reacted accordingly when someone chimed in. Her attention-to-detail made me closely aware of her thoroughness and I appreciated how the time flew. Before I noticed, we were standing giving her an ovation and calling for more. Bravo and Encore!

She made us laugh and she made people feel and she left me wanting to know much to rent out the space for the night. It was awe-inspiring. I was titillated, I was turned on. Suddenly in that moment I envisioned myself and welcomed the thoughts that followed. I was engaged, I was immersed. My future is mine, and if I'm going to have a good one, I'm going to have to

135

get involved instead of letting life happen.

I couldn't wait to get home from the show. I picked up writing where I left off. First, I needed to remove all distractions and turned off my screens. I researched publishers and made a quick decision to finish what I started. I wanted to acknowledge Reishon for telling me to take my dreams off hold and pursue them with great passion. When I saw her, I saw me. I decided to thank her and Ayvette in the book. Ayvette has encouraged me, tremendously, to get off my ass and travel the world.

Three days after my dream about Ayvette and her husband, she texted me, "I'm in New Jersey..." After ten years, we decided to meet at the Jay-Z exhibit at the Brooklyn Public Library. (Jay-Z is now noted as the richest musician in history. Estimated 2.5 billion dollars. Go head, Sir.)

Jay-Z sings in his freestyle for "Grammy Family": "Please may words be recorded to serve as testimony that I saw it all before it came to fruition, sort of a premonition, uncontrollable Hustler's Ambition. Alias Superstition, like Stevie. The writings on the wall like my lady, right baby? Saw it all before, some of y'all thought I was crazy, maybe."

Ayvette's son has writing credits in the exhibit. Aaron, born in 1991, wrote and directed the words used in the exhibit and spoken by Angie Martinez. His work as a writer has impressed many.

All in attendance received a Book of HOV. I was a little disappointed we were unable to get the commemorative library card because we were out-of-state. Unbeknownst to me, Ayvette was accompanied by her mother, who I haven't seen since the late 90's and she also invited Reishon. Just two days ago, I dedicated my work to these same ladies. I was aghast. I was so blessed to have this day.

We were able to view the exhibit, update each other on what's new and laugh about old high school memories. I really wish we had invited Kisha, Stephanie and Dawn. They all live in Brooklyn and after seeing us on FaceBook said, they were just there. It would've been nice to reunite with all the girls from the Drama Department.

In the middle of the library there was a replica of Jay-Z's recording studio.

Once inside we challenged Reishon to recite a few lyrics. My favorite line was when she said, "Fellas know me in the streets as Staxx/ and they wanna show off, pull out their greenbacks/ I roll in a Jag, cream interior/ I stay in a fur, keep fellas inferior/ Yo! You can't mess with a Harlem chick/ Independent woman, hardly a trick/ I sleep in cash, keep a fast stash, go head, and act up/ it's shorty on the dash..." She had the whole place involved and her performance warranted an applause.

All day we took pics in the library, right outside, later on getting ice cream from the Mister Softee truck, and with our sons and mom in the middle. Ayvette and I admired each other's loc length, and she complimented my face-framing bob. Just the night before I shampooed, deep conditioned, retwisted, slept in clips with a head wrap so I could live in this moment and say, "Oh! These old things? Thanks girl!" Friends for over thirty years but I'm positive no one in attendance would've guessed we were older than thirty-seven.

We ended our day at dinner. Some little soul food spot, Aaron recommended. Her mom and I sat close to catch up. She was pleased with the work she had done on the house in Jamaica. She took out her phone to show me pictures and right at that moment I felt like I was eavesdropping when Ayvette and Reishon broke into their own conversation. Through mom's pictures and story about renovating, I heard Ayvette admit she and her husband had gotten a divorce shortly after the wedding. I politely excused myself from mom because it was the first time I heard about this, and I wanted to ask a question. I stopped myself from judging and listened. She confessed he put hands on her. I cringed at the thought and blurted out, "No red flags?"

"Yea...but I made them pink." She said with a sneer.

It profoundly saddened me to hear this about my friend and mentor. Later that night, I sat in silence, closed my eyes, and breathed deeply.

I envision myself hosting a fundraiser for men and women stuck in domestic violence. I stand in front of a crowd full of black and brown people with advanced degrees and portfolios to make a difference. I need water to quell the butterflies in my stomach, but I am confident. I am lightly misted in Baccarat Rouge 540 and wearing a yellow suit dress by LaQuan Smith, simple silk blouse, and ballet flats. My waist-length locs are pulled up in a loose bun. I am surrounded by the likes of Shondra Rhimes, Ava DuVernay, Issa Rae, Regina King, Tracee Ellis Ross, and Celeste Ng. I am heading a foundation to aid, educate, and create a bridge to the next step. It's called: How to Leave. Domestic Abuse. My focus is safety and I hope, in some minuscule way, to make an impact.

I clear my throat as I am called up to the podium, "Please welcome Sunny Dandridge to the stage." The thunderous applause electrifies me, and the sea of faces make me super-charged. I adjust the microphone and take a deep breath. I thank the audience for coming and, "I couldn't have done this without you." I pause for another breath and dramatic effect. My voice is amplified through the speakers and around the hall. I can be heard down the stairs and outside of the charity event to this little girl standing at the bus stop. My words resonate. I'm smiling in my dreams. "Stop looking at how others live their life. Live yours. Love your life and make your mess your message." My insides are vibrating, and I hum with the visual.

At one of my local book signings, I am approached by Reed Hastings' assistant. My heart feels like it skipped a beat, but I reassure myself this is where I am meant to be. They offer me a deal with Netflix, eight episodes to start. I am extended a seven-figure deal. I add Executive Producer and Lead Writer to my credits. In the contracts, I insist that 60-75% of the cast and crew are black and brown. I smell chocolate chip cookies baking. I negotiate future book deals for the prequel and the next chapter.

I am able to reach young black men, young white men, and women everywhere. They all write me letters of thanks. I can tell it's about time we stop hiding the scars and live in our truth.

Travels to Ghana, Kenya, and Nairobi are yearly. The houseboat on the coast of San Pedro, Belize is my winter getaway.

Thank you. Thank you. Thank you. This is wonderful. How good can it get?

I take a long exhale and open my eyes.

Late September

The third time I ran into Reishon was at the CryOut Cave in Newark.

Her partner/ director of her show hosts here monthly. I rehearsed one of my pieces from four years ago.

No Ordinary (A Poem)

LOUD SIREN NOISE-LOUD SIREN NOISE-LOUD SIREN.

This is a TEST of the EMERGENCY Broadcast system... This. Is. ONLY. A. TEST.

You jumped up from behind the bed and yelled, "SUR-PRISE!" And quickly threw confetti in my eyes as I step back to see where the rest of the party was. You jump ahead two weeks and tell me where I eat, sleep and live. Got my exact hand motions down as I ask, "And where the hell you been?!"

Didn't know I was so predictable but wasn't your mouth that moved and first spoke of house keys? But GO head, give them to me. See what I might do. Might just hand them shits right back to you, might just give them to a homeless man looking for room and board. Might just come home one day smelling like fried chicken and collard greens, mashed potatoes and black eye peas, cornbread, and pecan pie, but no.

That would be the stamp on the envelope of the letter that read, "I DON'T WANT ANYONE ELSE but YOU." What a horrible thought that would be, to be tied down and labeled?! I don't want you waking up in cold sweats screaming, "NO! WHAT DID I DO?!" As I sleep laying next to you. I'm not the type of chick that says, "Nothing comes between me and my Calvins."

You need space to breathe and room to roam?

All this yours (waving hand in the air), all this is yours (waving hand to the left), ALL THIS? (Hand on crotch) ...is a test for richer for poorer. This is a test for sickness and in health. This is a test for better life expectancy. See? Where I eat, sleep, and live we got much love to give. But much to my surprise you want this love in disguise. Can't camouflage all this... here.

(In my Sade singing voice) "This. is. no. Or-din-ary love, No ordinary love."

This is no ordinary love cause I'm no ordinary chick. Must have me confused with some ordinary, run-of-the-mill, only-love-on-the-weekend type bitch.

Know what? Say less. You can't handle this...

I walk off stage feeling refreshed and exhilarated. I hadn't been to an open mic in all that time, call it COVID. Before the pandemic, I enjoyed the Nuyorican Poets Cafe on the Lower East Side, monthly. The Show, Words was hosted by my favorite twins, Gaston and WiseGuy (Class of '92); my Hip Hop Historians. They received an Emmy nomination in 2022 for their spoken word on CBS Sports' "Celebrating Black Stories" series.

Reishon and I were able to have a one-on-one. She revealed to me I was named Spring in her memoir, as I had a part in her meeting Big Daddy Kane in high school. We laughed as she recalled the story. Call it fate, destiny, kismet, divine intervention, or the Holy Spirit; I was touched by her words and brought to tears. I was overwhelmed with the feeling of purpose.

I went home to introduce the book release to the boys. They nodded in agreement; this was a good thing. I made mention I would be airing out my dirty laundry and my past would be on display for all to see. They paused, asked questions as they should, but continued to encourage me to live in my truth and not to worry about what other people say. "What about those who will laugh and go, 'Ah ha—your mom!'?" Cue shook his head and repeated, "Those people don't matter." We shared a moment in our family group hug. We made sure to pick up Winslow because he loves being included. I thank them again for knowing my heart and loving me in spite of my flaws.

September 25th

(The beat drops for Bent by Kyle Rich x Jenn Carter x TaTa x MCVERTT.)

6:02pm

Hey!

How have you been

Well look at u lookin how u
lookin lol

So whats up

U still don't smoke? I was
thinking about you earlier

Nah I really stopped
sometimes edibles

How much do you pay for
those?

Around 50-55

And I miss chilling with u

Really?
So sweet!

And I'm sure I can get them cheaper and better quality

Always the salesman Miss u too

Well can I come hang out with you again

I hope it goes without saying that I miss that pussy on a real grown woman who knows what she wants and to this day no one does it the way that you do

Lol I hope that's good

I would love to snuggle with you My sons are here

😵 I heard from you I'm very comfy to snuggle with but I know at least one of your kids doesn't want to see me LOL and now he got military training and I'm old LOL

Yea old, 30? lol

I'll be 30 in 2 months

I just turned 50

If I didn't know u I would never believe that

You free tonight? I can't have sex tho

I got work tomorrow so i gotta go to bed soon but why can't u have sex

I'm saving myself for my husband Haven't had sex in months He's coming I'm patient

144

Lol oh really

So u don't miss the way I
make love to you at all?

> Do you remember
> that party Ben had
> in his basement?
> I was fucked up

When you molested me and
told Ben to go back inside
Lol

> Lol you loved every
> minute of that shit I
> still think of you it's
> true

No you loved it because I
always saw you as attracted
to me LOL but you being
fucked up made you slick
and use patting me down
for coke as a reason to feel
my body. Plus you told me
you were scared of Tabitha

She's admittedly crazy, right?

I agree but she was fuckin Ben and a few others. I don't know if they was fucking when you and him were together but they was definitely fucking when y'all broke up while her & I were still together she was spending nights with the kids at his house and not telling me. Then Ben got lit and admitted to me while at the same time trying to apologize because he didn't know me and her were serious

I wanna remind you that this here for you when

Want to get married?

Maybe

I haven't seen him since 2021. We occasionally speak and we follow each other on IG.

September 26th

Donald Trump is found guilty of fraud for inflating his assets in a civil case brought on by New York Attorney General Letitia James. (65)

September 27th

The Hollywood writers' strike ends. Mitchell Marchand (Class of '91) posts on his FB timeline: A picture of him smiling and posing in front of a "CLOSED SET" sign. The next post: A GRAMMY Salute to 50 Years of HIP HOP: "Wednesday night was a vibe. Catch it December 10th on CBSTV It's for all of us who love Hip Hop. We gave flowers to all. Proud to have been a part of it and work with Nefetari Spencer and David Wild along with my folks Jesse Collins Ent. #WrittenBy #HeIsBack

Mitchell's line in the 1992 movie "Juice" starring Tupac and Omar Epps, is the most memorable: "Yo...You got the juice now, man" End credits.

September 28th

Kerry Washington, Bronx native, hands out her new memoir Thicker Than Water on the F train as her image on the cover of RUE Magazine adorns my side table.

September 29th

Trailblazing California Senator Dianne Feinstein dies at ninety. She was the longest-serving female senator. (66)

Omar Epps promotes his book Nubia: The Awakening on The Breakfast Club. (Class of '90) one sound bite that resonates, "Let's transform our traumas into superpowers." I recommend his memoir, From Fatherless to Fatherhood to my sons.

October

National Depression and Mental Health Screening and ADHD Awareness Month and so much more...

October 1st

Happy Heavenly Birthday, Edna Elizabeth Smaw Knight. Born in 1910, Gaga would have been 103 today. May her name live on in history books.

October 2nd

Simone Biles nails the Yurchenko double pike vault at the world championships—which will be named after her (five skills total will be named Biles). She helped secure a record seventh world team title. (67)

Her story is written, yet again, when Laphonza Butler is sworn into the senate, replacing Feinstein. She is the first Black openly LGBTI senator in American history. (68)

October 3rd

The cover of Esquire features Yusef Salaam and the Act of Forgiveness. As one of the Central Park Five, he served seven years in prison for a horrific crime he didn't commit. Now he wants to serve the city that condemned him. He says, "I'm dedicating my life to being useful. To my community, to my neighborhood, to my city. And that means letting go of some burdens of the past. Never forgetting but forgiving. There is power in forgiving." He was a sophomore at LAG in 1989 (honorary class of '91).

October 12th

Questlove is given the honor as Executive Director for "A GRAMMY Salute to 50 Years of Hip-Hop."

October 15th

Cue picked up the Bible and started going to church on Sundays asking for salvation. He has a TikTok and IG dedicated to spreading the word of God. Now in our disagreements I ask him, "What would Jesus do?" It stops him for a second so we can agree it's better to always do the right thing. As we forgive those who trespass against us, and we ask for forgiveness for our trespasses. I never thought I'd see the day I was quoting scripture. But in the crazy mixed up scheme of things God has sent him to me. I am truly blessed. He taught me not to think of it as a religion but a relationship with God, prayer as a conversation, and reading the Bible as learning. Lord knows I have a lot to learn. I thank him in my conversations and look to strengthen my relationship.

Mom asked about my writings yesterday. I read her a few excerpts; she loved them and requested I write more. (I didn't tell her about the book publishing, I wanted it to be a surprise.) In turn, Mom read a poem she wrote entitled "Monique." I confessed Mo likes to tickle my right elbow at night and sometimes puts a blade of grass in my ear like when we were little.

I saw her today. She's actually here with me now....here in my heart.

CHAPTER ELEVEN

I am who I believe myself to be. I am an accomplished writer. I am an amazing actress and a heterogeneous stylist. I am a teacher and a student. I am a professional artist and a lifetime dreamer. I am a motivational speaker and a dormant dominatrix. I am a mom and sister, daughter, and a friend. I am an auntie and a beautiful Black woman with a story to tell. I believe I was given gifts to share and given lessons to shape who I am. I am a fierce competitor and a fragile child.

I forgive myself for being broken. I say I love you to the image in the mirror before I lie in my bed tonight, I count one hundred and two locs and breathe deeply. I can hear myself, but I rarely heed myself. Congratulations, Sunny, for finishing what you started. After I get what I've manifested, I ask for the discipline to keep it and the wisdom to multiply it.

I feel it's my responsibility to break the generational curse of sweeping "lost and confusion" under the rug. It is our time to talk about the ills of Uncle Fred, the wrongdoings of Cousin Chris and the tainted demeanor of the babysitter. I dream of a day when "come healed" is a given and not just an euphemism.

I close my eyes and take a deep... Wait! What the fuck is that?! ...By the sound of it, my upstairs neighbors are dancing to "Bongos" or jumping on the bed with their shoes on? I squint to hear better and cock my head to the side for a more in-depth investigation. Sounds... like... somebody's definitely polishing the headboard. One moaning and a position change later I'm like, Get it, sis! Lord knows I'm not getting any. A little jealous and a little disgusted, I turn to readjust my pillows real hard maybe drown out the noise because who the fuck can sleep with all the...wait? ... They're finished? Damn, that was quick. I laugh is a "Pssst" and a loud, "HA!"

I close my eyes......

Heavenly Father,

May my worst days be praised because it could've been my last and may my best days be filled with gratitude, reflecting on my past. Every trial and tribulation was meaningful and appreciated. Thank you for the strength to stand tall and try again. The courage to move forward after failed attempts, the discipline not to retract and the grace to love me through my sins.

As I take a step back to reflect on my life, I become aware of the cravings we not only have for food but for desires not within your purpose. You are my peace, protector, and provider in a world where I am sometimes lost. Clear my vision and let me not overshadow my needs for once. Help me withstand temporary satisfaction for everlasting fulfillment.

May I stay close to you through the storms and the sunshine because my time aligns with God's time.

In Jesus' name, we pray. Amen.

My peace, protector, and provider @thatspatb2

AFTER THOUGHTS

I write to you so you can put down your judgements and learn. Maybe if we better understand each other, we can better love each other. It's not race or color that divides us; it's our culture and class. If you don't understand, ask, learn, accept, and grow. We are the colors of the rainbow. We need each other to shine.

I would like to thank everyone who took this ride with me. I hope you see yourself in me.

I like to think I'm speaking for everyone, even though I know I'm speaking for myself. This is my story and my journey. My intentions were to touch you. When I speak to everyone, I know I may also be speaking to someone who puts their hands on a family member or child or significant other. And to that percentage, I'd like to say, your hurt doesn't have to be someone else's. Your pain doesn't have to propel you to hurt and openly abuse. You can heal; you can forgive. For anyone who has the propensity to act out in violence and use their fists or words to put the person next to you down: you are better than that. Deep down in your soul, you strive to be in control of your emotions. If you are in that percentage of people I'm talking to, research your past and learn from it. I thank you for making me stronger, but I'm going to need you to acknowledge yourself as we move forward. Think about how you want to be perceived as we leave our bookmark in this mere history book. Do unto others as you would have done to your grandma: with love and gentle kindness.

I've exposed myself to you so that someone can hear me. If you are at the hands of a person who is making you feel bad most of the time or telling you that you're not enough, your time is now. Make a plan, write it down, keep it secret, hold everything tight until the time comes. Have a backup plan if that doesn't work, have money saved, let people know that you're in danger and you need to get out. Once you leave an abusive relationship, don't go back!

Don't allow your kids to grow up and see their parents ostracized and belittled. Better yet, don't have children with someone who is already showing you signs.

Come out from hiding, little one; the game of hide and seek is over. The game is a façade. You should never hide. Seek your true self. Find out who you are and what you're made of and how strong your backbone is and how your word is born. Challenge yourself to be greater.

I still hurt from my decisions and indecisions, from my "what if" and "why him" to "why am I here?" I wrench deeply inside my soul to understand: why? But I do know why the caged bird sings.

Lamb on Missy Elliot's song, "I'm Better" sings, "I'm going to start from the bottom/ Show you how to flip a dollar/ I got food in my dining room/ I'm better, I'm better, I'm better/ It's another day another chance/ I wake up I want to dance/ So as long as I got my friends/I'm better, I'm better, I'm better."

"Let the weak say, I AM STRONG." Joel 3:10

April 5th 2021

The last prayer by DMX on The Breakfast Club

"Let us pray. Father God, we thank you for this gathering of souls. See, when two or more gather in your name, we have your presence. Thank you for your presence. We pray for your grace and blessings upon us this day. We pray that you guide us, and, after, you have your will, and you have your way in our lives. We pray that any obstacle the devil has planned to place in our path be removed in the name of Jesus. We thank you, Father, for the many blessings you have given us so far. The food we have to eat, the clothes we have to wear, the cars we have to drive, the money we have to spend, and the lives we have touched, and the lives that touch our own. We pray, Lord, that we're able to stay focused and not be distracted by the obstacles the devil places in our path. We thank you, Lord, for your mercy, your grace, and your blessings. In Jesus' name, we pray. Amen."

THANK YOU with much respect.

LOVE me.

NOTES

Articles of interest:

From The Trace.org -Investigating Gun Violence in America

Dangerous homes: *Guns and Domestic Violence extract a deadly toll on kids. Most parents worry a shooting could happen at their children's school, but a Trace analysis found that* ***three times as many kids were shot in Domestic Violence*** *incidents between 2018 and 2022.*

   Jennifer Mascia

An Atlas of American gun violence: *9 years, 330,000 shootings. How has gun violence marked your corner of the country?*

   Daniel Nass

One of America's favorite handguns is allegedly firing on its owners: *Sig Sauer's P320 pistol has wounded more than 80 people who they say didn't pull the trigger—and now no U.S. agency has the power to intervene.*

   Champe Barton and Tom Jackman

How often are AR style rifles used in self-defense? *Supporters of AR-15s, often used in mass shootings and racist attacks, say they're important for self-defense. Our analysis of Gun Violence Archive data suggest otherwise.*

   Jennifer Mascia

RESOURCES

Substance Abuse and Mental Health Administration's 24/7 National Helpline: 1-800-662-HELP

Domestic Abuse Helpline for Men and Women: 1-800-7HELPLINE

Safe Haven (Support for Families dealing with Gun Violence): 1-866-869-HELP

Why Does He do That: Inside the Minds of Angry and Controlling Men written by Lundy Bancroft

To help my sons avoid these common misunderstandings of love I share this with them, and I also share with you.

According to the **National Center for Domestic and Sexual Abuse,** *here are some:*

Warning signs of domestic violence or "RED FLAGS":

Does your partner tease you in a hurtful way in private or in public?

Does your partner call you names such as "bitch" or "stupid"?

Does your partner act jealous of your friends, family, or coworkers? Does your partner get angry about clothes you wear or how you style your hair?

Does your partner check up on you by calling, driving by, or getting someone else to?

Has your partner gone places with you or sent someone just to "keep an eye on you"?

Does your partner insist on knowing who you talk to on the phone?

Does your partner blame you for their problems or their bad mood?

Does your partner get angry so easily that you feel like you're "walking on eggshells"

Does your partner hit walls, drive dangerously, or do other things to scare you?

Does your partner often drink or use drugs?

Does your partner insist you drink or use drugs with them?

Have you lost friends or no longer see some of your family because of your partner?

Does your partner accuse you of being interested in someone else?

Does your partner read your mail or go through your stuff or your other personal papers? Does your partner keep money from you, keep you in debt, or have "money secrets"?

Does your partner keep you from getting a job or cause you to lose a job?

Has your partner sold your car, made you give up your license, or not repaired your car?

Does your partner threaten to hurt you, your children, family, friends or pets?

Does your partner force you to have sex when you don't want to?

*Does your partner force you to have sex in ways that
you don't want to?*

*Does your partner threaten to kill you or himself if
you leave?*

*Is your partner like Dr. Jekyll and Mr. Hyde, acting one way in front
of other people and another way when you're alone?*

SAY THEIR NAME

Say his name… George Floyd
Say her name… Breonna Taylor
How many others do you know?

George Perry Floyd Jr. *(October 14, 1973- May 25, 2020) was an American man who was murdered by a White police officer in Minneapolis, Minnesota, during an arrest made after a store clerk suspected Floyd may have used a counterfeit twenty-dollar bill. Derek Chauvi, one of the four police officers who arrived on the scene, knelt on Floyd's neck and back for 9 minutes and 29 seconds, causing his death from lack of oxygen.*

George was a human being placed on this Earth for a reason.

Tamir E. Rice *(June 25, 2002- November 22, 2014), a 12-year-old American boy, was killed in Cleveland, Ohio, by Timothy Loehmann, a 26-year-old police officer. Rice was carrying a replica toy gun; Loehmann shot him almost immediately upon arrival on the scene. Loehmann's response was found to be "a reasonable one" since Tamir's toy gun did not have an orange tip.*

Tamir was a child of God; missed deeply by his mother, father, sister, and brother.

Philando Castile *(July 16, 1983- July 6, 2016) was a 32-year-old American man, fatally shot by police officer Jeronimo Yanez of the St. Anthony police department in the Minneapolis- Saint Paul metropolitan area. Castile was driving his girlfriend, and their four-year-old daughter, when he was pulled over. He informed officer Yanez he was licensed to carry a firearm and he was armed. After telling Castile several times not to pull it out, Castile confirmed multiple times "I'm not pulling it out". The police officer then fired seven close-range shots at Castile, hitting him five times. Yanez was fired from the police department but acquitted of all charges.*

Philando was a law-abiding citizen. His family is outraged and rightfully so.

Eric Garner (September 15, 1970- July 17, 2014) was a 43-year-old American man killed in the New York City borough of Staten Island by Daniel Pantaleo, NYPD officer. Pantaleo put him in a chokehold while arresting him on suspicion of selling single cigarettes. His death sparked outrage because in the video of his death he can be heard saying, "I can't breathe," 11 times while lying face down on the street. A Richmond County grand jury decided not to indict the officer responsible.

Eric was a husband, a father, grandfather and known as the "neighborhood peacemaker."

Breonna Taylor (June 5, 1993- March 13, 2020) was an American woman who was shot and killed while unarmed in her Louisville, Kentucky home by three police officers who entered under the auspices of a "no-knock" search warrant. After Louisville Metro Police Department ex-detective Brett Hankison was acquitted of felony wanton endangerment of Taylor's neighbors at the state level; Attorney-General Merrick Garland announced the Department of Justice was charging Hankison with unconstitutional use of excessive force that violated Taylor's civil rights.

Breonna was a daughter, a sister, and a friend. May she forever spark the conversation for change.

Sandra Annette Bland (February 7, 1987- July 13, 2015) was a 28-year-old American woman who was found hanged in a jail cell in Waller County, Texas, three days after being arrested during a traffic stop. Bland was pulled over for a minor traffic violation on July 10th by State Trooper Brian Encinia. The exchange escalated, after she refused to put out her cigarette, resulting in Bland's arrest and a charge of assaulting a police officer. After authorities reviewed the dashcam footage, Encinia was placed on administrative leave for failing to follow proper stop procedures. Her cause of death is still highly disputed.

Sandra spoke out against police brutality and demanded civil rights for people that looked like her.

Bill number S.B. 1849

The Sandra Bland Act addresses how law enforcement will be trained, jails will be equipped and what resources will be available to people with mental illness, substance abuse or intellectual differences.

The events leading up to Sandra Bland's unnecessary jailing and tragic death sparked statewide and national outrage.

hostontx.gov/txlege/sb-1849-sandra-bland-act

Tanisha Anderson, was a 37-year-old American woman who died in 2014 in Cleveland, Ohio after her family repeatedly called 911 for mental health assistance. She was bipolar and schizophrenic. But instead of help, police handcuffed and slammed Tanisha face down on an icy sidewalk. She later died in the hospital. Her family still fights to have "Tanisha's Law" passed to help educate police on mental health patients' needs.

Tanisha was a human being with a family and friends who miss her daily. May her death be a reminder: we all matter.

cleveland.com/metro/2014/11/cleveland_woman_with_mental_illness

Atatiana Koquica Jefferson (November 28 1990- October 12, 2019) a 28-year-old American woman was fatally shot inside her home by police officer Aaron Dean in Fort Worth, Texas. One of her neighbors called the police reporting Jefferson's front door was open. Police body camera footage shows them walking around the house with flashlights and one yells, "Put your hands up! Show me your hands!" while discharging his weapon through her kitchen window. Officer Dean resigned and he was indicted on murder charges but no conviction.

The Atatiana Project was started by her 8-year-old nephew, Zion, who witnessed the murder, to demand justice. Atatiana was an avid gamer, an auntie, and loved deeply by family and friends.

justiceforatatiana.com (sign the petition)

Just to name a few...Please keep their memories alive.

All memories are thanks to Wikipedia except Tanisha Anderson, she's remembered by cleveland.com.

According to media sources, police shot and killed 1,153 people in 2023.

Black people were disproportionately impacted by the use of lethal force, comprising nearly 18.5% of deaths from police use of firearms, despite representing approximately 13% of the population.

Following a visit by the UN International Independent Expert Mechanism to Advance Racial Justice in the Context of Law Enforcement, the delegation called on the USA to collect, compile, analyze and publish data, disaggregated by race or ethnic origin, on direct interactions by the population with law enforcement and the criminal justice system. It also required the USA to ensure accountability in all cases of excessive use of force and other human rights violations by law enforcement officials, through prompt, effective and independent criminal investigations, with a view to holding perpetrators accountable.

On 18 January, a multi-agency law enforcement operation led by Georgia State Patrol officers started to clear encampments of Defend the Forest activists, who had been camped in the forest on the outskirts of Atlanta, Georgia, since late 2021 to prevent the development of Cop City. Official accounts claimed officers came across a tent and verbally ordered the person inside to exit. Officers claimed that the person inside the tent, Manuel Esteban (Tortuguita) Páez Terán, an environmental human rights defender, shot at the officers, allegedly injuring a state trooper, before the officers returned fire and killed them. An independent autopsy revealed that Páez Terán had been shot 57 times and failed to find gunpowder residue on their hands.

amnesty.org/location/americas/noth-america

We, the people, demand better.

REFERENCES

Introduction

1. hypebeast.com/2023/11/wu-tang-clan-honorary-day-new-york-city

2. revolt.tv/article/2023-12-14/345708/KRS-One-explains-why-he-didnt-take-part-in- grammys-Hip-Hop-tribute

3. abcnews.go.com/US/mass-shootings-days-2023-database-shows/story?id=96609874

4. Law Enforcement Epidemiology Project, School of Public Health, "U.S. Data on Police Shooting and Violence," University of Illinois Chicago

Chapter 1

5. nytimes.com/2020/01/26/sports/basketball/kobe-bryant-dead

6. Wikipedia

7. nasa.gov/centers-and-facilities/langley/katherine-johnson-biography

8. nytimes.com/article/breonna-taylor-police

Chapter 4

9. Wikipedia

10. bmj.com/company/newsroom/fatal-police-shootings-of-unarmed-black-people-in-us-more-than-3-times-as-high-as-in-whites/

11. nytimes.com/202/07/17/us/john-lewis-dead

12. cnn.com/2021/07/27/sport/simone-biles-toyko-2020-olympics/index

Chapter 5

13. nytimes.com/2020/08/28/movies/chadwick-boseman-dead

14. supremecourt.gov/about/biographyginsburg

15. democrats.senate.gov/newsroom/press-releases/schumer-

floor-remarks-on-president-trump-refusing-to-condemn-the-white-supremacist-group-proud-boys

Chapter 6

16. revolt.tv/article/2020-11-06/66483/king-von-passes-away-in-atlanta

17. inquirer.com/politics/election/trump-says-concede-electoral-college-votes-biden-20201126.html

Chapter 7

18. nul.org/news/kizzmekia-corbett-african-american-woman-praised-key-scientist-behind-covid-19-vaccine

Chapter 8

19. nytimes.com/2021/01/13/us/politics/trump-impeached.html

20. hollywoodreporter.com/news/music-news/dmx-new-york-rapper-and-actor-dies-at-50

21. Wikipedia

22. npr.org/2022/02/18/1081597518/kim-potter-daunte-wright-sentencing

23. Wikipedia

24. Wikipedia

25. nyc.gov/office-of-the-mayor/news/423-003/emergency-executive-order-423

26. Wikipedia

27. Wikipedia

28. Wikipedia

29. cbsnews.com/news/biden-obama-clinton-911-new-york-display-of-unity/

30. Wikipedia

31. Wikipedia

32. Wikipedia

33. semons.love/joel-osteen "A New Mindset"

34. indiewire.com/features/general/bridgerton-season-2-netflix

35. nytimes.com/2022/04/18/arts/music/dj-kay-slay-dead

36. people.com/parents/all-about-rihanna-asap-rocky-son

37. judiciary.senate.gov/judge-ketanji-brown-jackson

38. nfl.com/videos/sandra-douglass-morgan-black-history-month

Chapter 9

39. https://www.businessinsider.com/memphis-city-councilman-breaks-down-over-tyre-nichols-footage-2023-1

40. Wikipedia

41. lvmh.com/news-documents/news/louis-vuitton-appoints-pharrell-williams-as-its-new-mens-creative-director/

42. Wikipedia

43. npr.org/2023/03/30/1164766452/trump-indictment-new-york-bragg-stormy-daniels

44. Wikipedia

45. Wikipedia

46. washingtonpost.com/politics/2023/07/19/trump-carroll-judge-rape

47. Wikipedia

48. washingtonpost.com/education/2023/05/24/florida-amanda-gorman-inauguration-poem

49. rmets.org/metmatters/worst-air-quality-world-wildfire-smog-smothers-new-york

50. abcnews.go.com/US/don-lemon-fired-cnn

51. radaronline.com/p/the-wire-co-creator-seeks-lenieency-drug-dealer-michael-k-williams

52. nytimes.com/2023/08/14/aarts/music/magoo-rapper-dead

53. people.com/parents/all-about-rihanna-asap-rocky-son

54. montgomeryadvertiser.com/story/news/local/2023/10/27/two-

white-boaters-plead-guilty-in-viral-montgomery-dock-brawl-case

55. Hill, Jahman Ariel. "Black History Month Fact #88,888: The Montgomery Brawl is a National Holiday" @jahman_rondo, 2024

56. cnn.com/2023/08/24/politics/donald-trump-surrender-fulton-county-jail-criminal-case

57. apnews.com/article/mug-shot-donald-trump-indictment-839920116a244df3e55bdedf33820a80

58. amsterdamnews.com/news/2023/10/10/nyc-declares-biz-markie-day

59. Biz Markie. "Just a Friend." *The Biz Never Sleeps,* 1989, Sony.

60. latimes.com/entertainment-arts/movies/story/2023-09-06/ava-devernay-venice-film-festival-first-african-american-woman

61. Mc Shan. "The Bridge." *Down By Law,* 1987, Bridge Records.

62. justice.gov/sco-weiss/pr/grand-jury-returns-indictment-charging-robert-hunter-biden-three-felonies-related-his

63. npr.org/2023/08/22/1195170311/shacarri-richardson-is-officially-the-fastest-woman-in-the-world

64. theguardian.com/fashion/2023/sep/18/chioma-nnadi-to-replace-edward-enninful-as-head-of-british-vogue

Chapter 10

65. forbes.com/sites/alisondurkee/2023/09/26/trump-commited-fraud-by-inflating-his-assets-judge-rules

66. apnews.com/article/dianne-feinstein-dead

67. nbcsports.com/olympics/news/simone-biles-vault-yurchenko-double-pike

68. cnn.com/2023/10/18/politics/laphonza-butler-senate-judiciary-committee

ABOUT AUTHOR

Sunny Dandridge was born in the Bronx, New York and raised in Queens, the same year as Hip Hop:1973. Born into poverty and she was raised to watch her back, carry carfare, and walk with rhythm for attitude and self-awareness. She is an innate "people watcher."

Sunny is a lifetime writer. Since childhood, she would write short stories and jot commercials down in her diary. While in junior high school she picked up a love for reading Stephen King and John Grisham novels. Her taste for poetry blossomed after she was introduced to Langston Hughes and Shel Silverstein. As a poet, she's performed on stages at the Nuyorican Poets Cafe in NYC and the Cry Out Cave in Newark, NJ.

She pursued acting very young at the Black Spectrum Theatre in Queens. She auditioned and was accepted to "FAME!" LaGuardia High School of Performing Arts in NYC and graduated in 1991. (Alongside Marlons Wayans, Omar Epps and Mitchell Marchand; the well-known comedian, acclaimed actor and prominent writer have remained friends until this day.)

After high school, she was exported to rural North Carolina. She let a shift in environment shift her immediate goal and enrolled in Carolina Beauty College, where she honed her third natural gift. She felt it was the death of any 18-year-old budding actress from New York City.

Sunny realized she had to choose one of her God-given gifts. Writing and Acting were put on hold because she never felt enough, so hair and make-up became the "thing to fall back on." She demanded top-of-the-craft professional training at Vidal Sassoon on 5th Avenue and 58th Street and then colorist training at the world-renowned Bumble and Bumble on 53rd and 3rd.

Sunny is quoted as saying, she is The Self-Proclaimed Hair Whisperer.

Her childhood home was rotted by domestic violence and since it felt natural, she allowed it to continue into her adulthood. Now she is a resident of northern

New Jersey and single-handedly reared her two sons, the Marine and the budding Fashion Designer. Ready to break the cycle for the next generation. Sunny sees a need for fresh education on the topic, an initiative to not to be afraid to speak up, and a demand to "cause a fuss."

Sunny's life changing event has compelled her to pen this memoir. In honor of the many we have lost due to COVID-19, gun violence and ex-police murders in the years of 2020- 2023.

Sunny is also in support of the Mental Health Narrative, Automatic Gun Control because Black Lives Matter and BLACK GIRLS ROCK!

Facebook: Sunny Dandridge

Instagram: Sunny_Dandridge

www.SunnyDandridge.com

www.ingramcontent.com/pod-product-compliance
Lightning Source LLC
La Vergne TN
LVHW052148121224
798984LV00057B/1729